FLY CAR

John H. Fuller

Fly Car

by John H. Fuller

Copyright @ 2014 by: John Fuller

Library of Congress Cataloging-in-Publication Data

Facebook Page: https://www.facebook.com/fullerflycar

Fly Car can also be purchased electronically through
Amazon....Key Words
Fly Car by John Fuller

To Hosanna, Sophie, and Jacquelline

the three women in my life who

make our house a home

Contents

Chapter 1

Busted

Slate gray clouds hovered in the sky like UFOs as Eli made his way down to his buddy's house. He and Earl Murphy had been best friends since second grade.

Murph's favorite hobby was trying to find creative ways to get out of school. His latest trick was mixing a little neon green sports drink, oatmeal, and water together until the concoction was at just the right consistency, then dumping it into the toilet. He'd wait for the exact moment when the contents began floating to the surface of the commode, then start moaning and groaning to his mom about not feeling well. But his secret sickness recipe had recently been discovered: his mom had found an empty crumpled-up Quaker Oats packet under his pillow.

Eli Martin, with his spiky brown hair, electric blue eyes, and below-average height, was quite a contrast to the larger-than-life Murph. Still, the boys had been best friends for as long as they could remember. Every weekday morning for the past three years, they had made the trek together to Thomas Edison Elementary School.

Their primary bond was that they both hated school. Actually, "hate" was too harsh, but "strong dislike" certainly described their feelings. Going through the same routine day after day made the underachieving pair feel as if their lives were on a constant rewind cycle.

Walking the neighborhood blocks toward Edison Elementary every day gave the boys an opportunity to talk about the day ahead and remind each other why they thought school was dumb. "Your attendance at school has been pretty solid lately," Eli said.

"Mom discovered my secret sickness recipe," said Murph. "I should have been more careful with the oatmeal packets."

"Murph, the secret sickness recipe is not exactly top secret. Kids have been pulling that trick for years. It was only a matter of time before your mom caught on."

"You're probably right."

The route from Murph's house to school took roughly ten minutes. This was Eli's favorite time of day. His mind would race through a million different ideas. He'd daydream, then take notes in his head and sock the best ideas away in a mental file cabinet of future possibilities.

Suddenly the first bell rang, startling Eli like an alarm clock waking him up from a really good dream.

Every morning the fifth-grade routine was the same: class attendance, followed by the Pledge of Allegiance, morning announcements, and the relentless yammering of the teacher. Sometimes Eli felt like a character trapped inside a *Peanuts* cartoon, with all the adult voices droning on in the same monotonous *wah wah wah* trombone tone for seven hours.

His current teacher was Mrs. Fitzgerald. Mrs. F was very nice, and at times interesting, but Eli's mind couldn't help but wander into another world that was more appealing to him than the confining four walls of the classroom. This world was one of vivid colors and dimensions and, most of all, inventions—fantastic machines and gadgets he dreamed up that could be useful in the near future, maybe even change the world for the better.

Mrs. F's voice closed in on Eli's daydream like a trap door, snapping him back into the reality of daily fifth-grade life. The closing school bell rang: 11:20 a.m. The kids quickly stacked their chairs and shuffled out of class.

Ten minutes later, Mrs. F was getting ready to meet with her students' parents for spring conferences. Eli's mom was first on the list.

Parent-teacher conferences were always the same story for Eli's mom. This year it was Mrs. Fitzgerald's turn to be the truth-teller, but his mom had heard the same thing from every one of his teachers: "Your son is bright, creative, and well liked by his peers, but he just doesn't seem motivated to do well in school."

This time she was ready with a response. "Why do you think that's so, Mrs. Fitzgerald?"

"I don't know.... I was hoping maybe you could tell me about your son's home life. It might help me get a clearer picture."

Eli's mom collected herself. "Well, as you know, times have been pretty tough around here since the economy headed south and crushed the auto industry," she said. "My husband, Michael, is CEO of Martin Motors. He's putting in some pretty long hours trying to salvage the company his great-grandfather founded back in 1931. He hasn't been at home too much lately."

In fact, Eli's mom didn't fully understand her own explanation. She'd always felt she should be able to do something more to help her underachieving son. But she'd never figured out what.

"I understand, I really do," Mrs. Fitzgerald said. "But Eli is starting to show some pretty significant gaps in his learning. He displays tremendous potential, but that needs to be matched with his overall performance."

"Any suggestions?" Eli's mom asked.

"He may need to attend summer school."

"Do you have a plan B?" Summer school would not change Eli, she knew; it would just be a pointless punishment.

"Let's see how he performs during the final trimester of the year before we do anything drastic," Mrs. Fitzgerald said.

After twenty minutes, Mrs. Fitzgerald and Eli's mom rose from their seats next to the teacher's desk, shook hands, and headed toward the classroom door. Mrs. F ended the meeting with a warm smile and her usual sign-off, "Thanks for coming in. Have a relaxing spring break."

Eli was waiting for his mom in the school's parking lot, near the family's black luxury sedan. As she unlocked his car door he looked at her quizzically, but she said nothing.

The ride home was very quiet until he decided to break the ice.

"So, how did it go?" he asked, feeling a little like an FBI agent interrogating a foreign spy.

"How did what go?" Mom said, pretending not to know what he meant.

"Come on, Mom, the parent-teacher conference. What did Mrs. F have to say?"

"She said you're a bright boy." Mom cracked a smile from the driver's seat.

"That all?" Eli hung on every word.

"Well, not exactly. She mentioned creative, well liked, and honest."

"Any bad news?" Eli probed.

"Does 'lacking personal organization and homework inconsistency' ring a bell?"

"That stuff is overrated." Eli replied dismissively, convinced of his own intelligence.

"That may be, but that 'stuff' could land you in summer school."

"It can't be that bad, can it?"

"You have one trimester to right the ship."

"And what if I sink, like the *Titanic*?"

"How does summer school sound?" Mom repeated, giving Eli a steely gaze.

"Two words: pure torture," Eli mumbled.

The sedan pulled into the driveway.

Chapter 2

Necessity's Boy

Martin Manor, where Eli lived, was the very definition of a manor. The sprawling estate included a chocolate-colored brownstone mansion, a meticulously groomed five-acre lawn complete with hedges squared off at ninety-degree angles, mature spruce and maple trees in all the right places, and an ivory-colored mermaid fountain at the center of a circular driveway. But even though his home looked like it could be featured on *MTV Cribs*, Eli never really felt comfortable there. To him, it didn't have the cozy feeling that a home should.

He'd felt the same way about a museum he'd visited on a school field trip. The museum had all the right pieces of art in all the right places, but at the end of the day he was eager to leave its stiff formality. He longed for the type of warm, casual, inviting home he saw on the cards his family got in the mail at the holidays. Martin Manor seemed desperately in need of a docent.

Eli's favorite part of the estate was a big old barn about a hundred yards behind the main house. It was one of the few original structures remaining from the days when his great-grandpa had acquired the property, in the early part of the twentieth century. The barn probably would have been demolished if the historical society hadn't discovered that the original Martin motorized vehicle was assembled there. Now it had been registered as a historic site and preserved.

It didn't look like much from the outside, with its classic red paint job and cream trim, but inside the barn was where dreams had come to life, according to Martin Motors legend. Sometimes Eli enjoyed coming out to the old barn just to soak up a little inspiration from its history and dream about what his own future might hold.

As the family sedan pulled up to Martin Manor, Eli noticed that Murph was camped out on his doorstep, thumbing through the baseball cards he always kept stashed away in his backpack. Murph popped up from his slouched position on the stoop and asked if Eli could play for a while.

"Sure," Mom said. It was the first Friday of spring break, and she was happy to be done with the parent-teacher conference. The boys sprinted at top speed toward the old barn with a sense of newfound freedom—freedom from school, freedom from Mrs. Fitzgerald's lessons and lectures, and freedom from the school routine that ruled their lives 180 days of every year.

The barn's double doors were fastened shut with a huge antique padlock to keep people out. It looked like the kind of lock that would guard Dr. Frankenstein's laboratory in a Saturday afternoon science fiction movie. Eli thought it would be cool to show Murph this mysterious place.

He reached for the iron key that was always hidden underneath the wooden red rooster just to the right of the barn doors. Shimmying the key into the keyhole and cranking it a quarter-turn clockwise, he felt the lock give way with a groan. The boys were able to pull the doors just wide enough to wiggle their way in.

Shafts of golden light entered the dark barn from an opening in the upstairs loft. The barn still gave off a pastoral

16

aroma after all these years, a reminder of its farm heritage. The smells of freshly cut grass and axle grease wafted through the boys' nostrils.

Eli watched as Murph caught sight of an object in the corner covered in a dusty cream-colored sheet, like a ghost from the barn's past. It wasn't a specter—the shape wasn't right—so it had to be something else. Curious, Murph pulled back the cover to reveal … a mint-condition cherry red sports car! His eyes nearly popped out of his head.

"Totally awesome ride!" he exclaimed.

Eli remembered his dad taking him to the barn a few years back to show him this prized possession, a 1984 Martin Mercurio. In fact, some of Eli's favorite memories were of times spent listening to his dad's stories of his teenage years spent driving around in the cherry red car. One story started off with his dad proudly earning his driver's license and being rewarded with a brand-new, just-off-the-assembly-line Martin Mercurio for his sixteenth birthday as a gift from his father. Young Michael was so excited that he piled in a couple of buddies from high school and drove nearly thirty miles north, to the nearest town with a drive-in movie theater, where the original *Ghostbusters* was showing.

Before the movie started, Michael decided to get some popcorn while the trailers rolled across the oversized sixty-foot outdoor screen. At the concession stand, he happened to meet a brand-new female employee in training—but not just any ordinary employee, a girl, and not just any girl, but The One. She was funny, flirty, and cute, and made Michael, who could be pretty introspective, come alive.

An hour later, he floated back to the Mercurio holding cold popcorn in one hand and warm drinks in the other. His buddies chided him for missing most of the movie, but he didn't care. He went back to the drive-in four more times that summer, making the thirty-mile trek just to see and talk to the girl behind the concession counter. Eventually he gathered up his courage and asked her on a date. She said yes—as long as it wasn't to see *Ghostbusters*.

A decade later, the girl at the popcorn stand would become Eli's mom. Before then there was high school graduation and college to attend, fraternity parties on Friday nights, and Michigan football games on Saturdays. But four years of university life passed quickly, and suddenly diplomas were handed out on a warm Saturday afternoon in June. One month later, Michael Martin and Megan Marshall had another ceremony to attend: they were married on a beautiful Midwestern afternoon, under blue skies, outside on the Martin Manor grounds. A simple reception in the barn followed, with barbecued ribs for dinner.

Eli held this story in his head like a movie. He loved every moment of his parents' courtship story. It was part of why he had such affection for the barn.

Murph, meanwhile, was experiencing a different love story: he was spellbound by the car. Almost thirty years later, the Mercurio still looked as if it had just come off the showroom floor. The boys spent the better part of an hour admiring it. They sat in the driver's seat, grasping the midnight black leather steering wheel, pretending to be

Formula One race-car drivers in Monte Carlo. Murph's heart thumped as he sat in pole position with the wheels hugging the crisp white starting line. The race was a back-and-forth contest as Eli provided the play-by-play commentating: "And it's neck-and-neck as the two cars slam down the straightaway…." Murph thought this was better than any version of Grand Prix Auto played on his video console.

Just as the checkered flag was about to drop, signaling victory for Murph, Eli heard a rustling noise that snapped him back to reality.

"Hello?" he said.

An elderly man in dusty blue coveralls, with a red handkerchief in his back pocket, suddenly appeared inside the dimly lit barn, ambling up to the car. He was a distinguished old-timer with skin the color of mahogany, more salt than pepper in his closely cropped curly hair, and a few wrinkles of wisdom mapping the corners of his eyes.

"Mmm, mmm, mmm … Sweet Ginger Brown sure don't make them like they used to." He looked admiringly at the car.

"Grady, what are you doing here?" Eli said.

"You forget, son. I am the cupbearer to the king, the keeper of the castle, the official officer. I am responsible for what happens on the grounds of Martin Manor." Grady put his leg up on a nearby crate.

"Oh yeah. I forgot," Eli countered.

"What are they teaching you two in school these days, boys?" Grady asked. The boys looked at each other.

"Nothing. Well, not really nothing, but boring stuff," Murph mumbled, and Eli nodded in agreement.

"Boring stuff? Now that's a darn shame." Grady shook his head back and forth, then clucked his cheeks. "Smart pair like you two should be having your minds catching fire, if you know what I mean. What's your favorite subject in school?"

"I like recess," Murph said.

"Recess isn't a subject, son."

"I like science. Especially when we get to complete experiments," Eli said.

"Why's that?" Grady asked.

"I like to solve problems in my mind—figure out puzzles, if you know what I mean."

"I think I'm starting to get the picture," Grady said. "Go on."

"In science you get to use trial and error. It's okay to make mistakes. Failure is acceptable as long as you learn from it," Eli said.

"The concept is called failing forward, Junior."

"That's it!" Eli squealed, as if he'd just found out he had a snow day.

"Have you ever learned how to make gadgets, Eli?" Grady's eyes started to sparkle like diamonds. "You know, use your mind to create inventions?"

"Only during Science Olympiad. It's my favorite week of school."

"What's Science Olympiad?" Grady asked.

"It's a really cool competition. You form small teams and invent things. Well, actually, there are different events. For example, one group tries to make boats out of clay that can hold the most metal washers before sinking." Eli was now very excited.

"I remember that," Murph said. "Our clay boat held thirty-eight washers and came in second last year!"

"Did you use Archimedes's law of water displacement?" Grady asked excitedly.

"What's that?" Eli inquired admiringly.

"Archimedes's story takes place 2,200 years ago, when the king of Syracuse requested that a certain jeweler design a crown for him out of a single bar of solid gold," Grady began.

"What does Archimedes have to do with clay boats?" Murph questioned.

"Not so fast, kid, we're getting to the good part. King Hieron suspected that the jeweler was taking a cut off the top by melting a less precious metal in with the gold to create the crown. He summoned Archimedes and ordered the great mathematician to create a way to prove his suspicions." Grady lowered his voice to hook his audience of two.

"So what did he do?" the boys asked in unison.

"Well, he noticed that water levels rise based on the density of the object placed in a container. You may have noticed this before. When you plop yourself into a bathtub, what happens?"

"The water level goes up, way up," Murph responded.

"Precisely. So all Archimedes had to do was place an identical bar of gold in a container of water and measure how much the liquid rose, then compare the water level when the crown was submerged in H_2O. If the water rose to the same level, then the jeweler had nothing to worry about. But Archimedes discovered that the water levels were not level to each other, making the jeweler …"

"… guilty as charged," Eli deduced triumphantly. "Just as the king suspected."

"What did you think of the story, Murph?" Grady quizzed.

"Interesting, but in our Science Olympiad we were just trying to keep our clay boat afloat," Murph said, looking a little confused.

"How about you, Eli? What competition did you participate in?" Grady asked.

"Aerodynamics."

"Tell me about that."

"Well, the goal was to design a paper airplane that can travel the farthest while still flying in a straight line through a positioned hula hoop." Eli remembered the event fondly.

"How far did you get the plane to travel?"

"I won. My airplane flew a distance of twenty meters and then floated right through the middle of the hoop," Eli said proudly

"What design did you use?" Grady probed.

"It's funny you mention that. Most people went with the traditional paper-airplane model—you know, the kind you learn how to make in first grade. But I created my own design."

"What was it?" Grady squinted his eyes as if he were trying to imagine the plane.

"My wings were positioned downward instead of upward," Eli replied.

"Why did you choose that design?" Grady was beginning to sound like a teacher, but Eli didn't mind.

"Well, I looked at quite a few airplanes, and many have wings that are at least level with the fuselage."

"That's good thinking, son."

"I aim to please," Eli quipped.

"Come here, boys," Grady said. "I want you two to have your own personal Science Olympiad. Look around the barn and find some items you could use to create a device— any kind you want. The only hitch is, you have just twenty minutes to make it."

"Any other rules?" Eli asked. The boys were alert and ready to go.

"Nope. But you're on the clock, so you'd better get cracking."

Eli's heart raced as he moved around the musty old barn. His mind sparked with excitement as he thought of the endless possibilities. Instinctively he grabbed for a dusty spare tire, some rope, and an old electric power drill. His mind's eye gave him a picture of Swiss cheese. He sparked up the old drill and excitedly started blasting hundreds of holes around the black rubber sidewalls of the tire.

Next he made four slightly larger holes that were equidistant from each other. These openings would serve as the anchor points for a rope, as in the tire swings he'd seen at neighborhood playgrounds. From there, he threaded some two-inch-thick twine through the holes and knotted the rope around the backside of the old rubber wheel. Finally, he took the four strands of tan rope and tied them into a point at the top vertex, like a vertical hammock.

"Done!" he said, smiling.

Murph, who had spent the better part of fifteen minutes climbing up an old wooden ladder and then jumping down from the loft onto an old pile of hay, scrambled to the corner of the barn and grabbed a twelve-foot black wrought-iron pole. "Me too."

Grady seemed unimpressed at Eli's invention. "What is it? Some kind of rope swing?"

"Come on, you'll see." Eli waved his arm and they all made their way over to the pond behind the barn. It was called Old Man Murphy's Pond—after a relative of Murph's, Eli knew, but he wasn't sure why.

At the water's edge, the boys took off their shoes and socks and flung them onto the grassy bank, then carefully rolled up their jeans to their knees and waded a few feet into the pond. The murky water became even cloudier as the boys' feet caused the mud to swirl up to the surface of the water like a whirlpool. Eli maneuvered through a series of cattails while Murph demonstrated his invention first.

"My invention is a depth finder," he said. "As you can see, the pond is exactly two and a half feet deep at this location." Just then, he slipped on a smooth, slippery stone and back-flopped into the pond with a splash. He popped up and immediately added, "I meant to do that. I was just confirming my results." Eli and Grady both smiled knowingly.

Meanwhile, Eli gently released the tire that hung around his shoulders and slowly submerged it underwater, allowing the sidewalls to gather the tea-brown translucent liquid from the pond. Quietly tiptoeing back to the shore, he held onto the twine like a seven-year-old clinging to a kite string for the first time. Silently, he waited for ten minutes while patiently squatting in a catcher's stance by the shore.

Grady began giving a local history lesson. "You know, it may not be such a coincidence that you two are such good buddies," he began.

"I'm not catching your drift," Murph said, nudging Eli.

"The Martins and the Murphys go way back, son. Your great-grandpa once owned this property back in the day. According to the history ledgers, Earl Murphy Sr. lost his fortune in the stock market crash of 1929, when he got in too deep purchasing blue chip stocks on margin."

"What does 'on margin' mean?" Murph asked.

"It was a way an investor could own an entire stock by paying only a small percentage of the price. It's a great financial strategy when stock prices are going up, but a disaster when they go down—which they did in 1929. They plunged, and Murph's grandfather was forced to sell this property to help pay off the debt he owed. And Eli, your great-grandpa purchased this parcel of land, including the pond, and renamed it Old Man Murphy's Pond as a tribute to his friend."

"Win some, lose some, I guess," Murph said.

Eli smiled.

Then he stood up and waded back into the cold, murky water up to his ankles. His feet quickly became numb. He grabbed the rope and pulled slowly, hand over hand, until his invention reemerged. Water drained out the sides of the tire as though cascading from a fountain.

Grady came in closer to inspect Eli's creation. As the tire continued to drain, something began to wiggle within the inner walls of the rubber.

"What is it?" Grady asked.

"A bass. Maybe a perch," Eli said.

"How did you know your invention would work?" Grady asked.

"Sometimes I get pictures in my mind of how an invention is supposed to work. This time it was a vision of

Swiss cheese. What's the first word that comes to your mind when I say 'Swiss cheese'?"

"Holes," Grady instantly replied.

"Exactly. So I made my design using that principle of holes to capture the fish in the tire. It's a concept that fishermen have used for centuries. I just reconfigured the tire into a modified fishing net."

Just then, Grady handed the boys the red rag from the back pocket of his overalls so they could dry off their soaking feet. "Not that this is going to do you much good, son," he said as he looked over at Eli's waterlogged best friend.

The mild spring day was moving toward dusk. Pink hues were transitioning to indigo as the sun dipped behind a willow tree that licked the edge of the pond.

"I have to get back to the house," Eli said. "My mom is still pretty upset over my report card, and I don't want to be grounded over spring break. Race you to the house, Murph!" Eli yelled as he sprinted across the endless lawn back toward Martin Manor. "Last one's a rotten egg!"

"No fair.... I'm soaking wet!" Murph took off after his best friend, but he was soon left in the dust.

"I'll be switched," Grady whispered under his breath. Rising to his feet, he gently snatched the hapless fish out of the tire and flipped it back into the pond with a plunk. The contact caused the glassy surface to ripple into an ever-expanding series of concentric rings—much like the shape of the tire, Grady thought, which, thanks to Eli's imagination, had become much more than an old piece of junk collecting dust in an oversized barn.

Chapter 3

Table for Two, Again

"I'm soaked!" Murph announced when they reached the door of Eli's house. "I'm going home to get dry. See ya tomorrow." He was off before Eli could say good-bye.

Eli flung open the door to the mudroom and heard his mom's voice from the kitchen: "Be sure to wash those dirty hands and rinse your face, Eli." Pre-meal etiquette was important to his mom, so he knew he'd better comply.

Meals in the dining room often gave Eli a weird feeling. It was odd to sit down at a formal table for eight and have only two people eating dinner, just him and his mom. It felt like they should be playing a game of chess, not sharing a family meal.

Eli missed his dad. He'd been hauntingly absent from dinners lately, as he was trying to give the Motor City a little economic tune-up. Detroit was an aging metropolis that was slowly becoming a modern-day ghost town. Once a manufacturing hub, this town, nearly overgrown with weeds, felt like a city that had lost its rhythm—not dead yet, but definitely on life support. His dad had once told Eli that it would take the city of Detroit until the year 2023 to fully recover from the economic downturn that began in 2008.

Eli decided to address the thought that he guessed was in his mom's mind.

"So, where's Dad?"

"Working late again," Mom said, pushing her flowing brown hair behind her ears in a nervous gesture.

"Trying to save the world?" Eli countered with a tinge of bitterness.

"I think he'd settle for keeping Martin Motors afloat." Mom gave Eli a pitcher of water to bring to the table.

All of a sudden, Eli exploded. "Why isn't Dad ever home for dinner? Is it too much to ask? Most kids in my class have a father who comes home for evening meals. I might as well make a cardboard cutout of Dad sitting in his spot at the table. At least that way, someone would be there."

"Your father is a very busy man these days," Mom said.

"Murph's dad is home for dinner when he isn't out of town on business." Eli stabbed at his food and then slammed down the fork.

"I know … I know. It just isn't that easy." She wanted Eli to drop the topic, but she didn't know what to say. Instead, she started wiping at an invisible spot on the table.

"What's so hard about showing up? Remember the Woody Allen quote you told me about, that 80 percent of life is just showing up? Can't I at least get 20 percent of his time? Is that asking too much?"

"I promise this season will pass, Eli," Mom pleaded. She reached out to touch his hand. Eli let her, then drew his hand away. He was gathering the courage to ask the question that he'd wondered about so many times.

"Does Dad love me? Does he even know that I exist?"

"Of course he does, Eli," she said reassuringly. "You probably don't know this, but two of the three biggest car companies in our country have filed for bankruptcy, and your dad's company isn't far behind. The city of Detroit just filed for bankruptcy too. Bankruptcy means they're all out of money."

"I know. Is it really that bad?" Eli asked, as a raindrop-size tear slid down his cheek.

"Your dad is working really hard so that won't happen to Martin Motors," she said.

"Can I help?"

Mom buried her head in her hands. "Can you make a car that runs on water?"

"Don't think so," Eli returned.

"How about a car that drives itself?"

"Google already figured that one out, Mom."

"Oh yeah, I read about that." She looked up at the chandelier, which had been there for almost a century. "How about a car that can actually fly?"

"You mean like a pod racer?"

"Kind of like that, but even higher. A car like that could revolutionize the auto industry!"

Eli got very quiet.

"But of course, that's impossible," she said.

Eli started to nod his head knowingly, then asked if he could excuse himself from the dinner table.

"But you hardly touched your food," Mom said.

"I've got some work to do. Good night." With that, Eli completed his second great disappearing act of the day.

Chapter 4

Freeways in the Sky

Bounding up the spiral staircase two steps at a time, Eli made his way to his bedroom and flopped onto the familiar twin bed. He gazed at the posters pinned to his ceiling: a midnight black Porsche Boxster, a sterling silver Mercedes Benz 450 SL, and a cherry red 1984 Martin Mercurio. Grabbing his brown leather-bound sketchbook from the desk next to his bed, Eli became introspective. He nervously clicked his mechanical pencil multiple times until the lead popped up, then started rapidly drawing: sketches, mostly. The flying concept intrigued him.

As he drew, conflicting thoughts and emotions raced through his mind at 100 miles per hour: bitterness and resentment at his dad for making him a D-level priority, inspiration from his fish-catching invention, and disappointment in himself for transferring his anger onto his mom.

Suddenly he was reminded of the day that Gene, Earl Murphy's father, had come to class to talk about his career as a commercial airline pilot. He described making trips across the vast Pacific Ocean to Tokyo, Japan. Mr. Murphy explained that when flying a commercial aircraft over a large body of water like the Pacific Ocean, the air traffic controller and pilot make up coordinates in the sky—places over the ocean where lines of longitude and latitude intersect to make imaginary points where no actual landforms exist below. The coordinates could have made-up names, like Simlu, Marlo, or Lyle. The planes take these same routes over and over again; they are like freeways in the sky. It doesn't matter if the flight is two hours long or ten; no sooner has one plane completed the pathway than another aircraft will take that exact course and eventually land at the same destination.

Eli knew this to be true; he'd studied the planes landing one after another on the lengthy runway at O'Hare Airport when he had a two-hour layover in Chicago. *Freeways in the sky, freeways in the sky, freeways in the sky*—the words rolled over and over in his mind. What if there actually were invisible freeways in the air, stacked one on top of the other, and vehicles that could travel not bound by the laws of gravity or traffic signals, but layered based on air space? There would be no more rush-hour traffic. Everyone would spend less time in cars, freed to live their lives. Parents could spend more time with their kids.

One last scene appeared in Eli's mind. The setting was a corner office overlooking downtown Detroit. A tired-looking corporate executive—Eli's dad—slowly took off his square black-rimmed spectacles and slid his hands through his salt-and-pepper hair. He loosened his tie, crossed his arms atop a large walnut desk, and proceeded to fall fast asleep. Just then, Eli's breathing fell into perfect cadence with that of his father's in the daydream.

A few hours later, Eli's mom slowly shuffled upstairs to check on her son. She saw that he'd fallen fast asleep, with the open sketchbook perched on his chest like a tepee. She gently removed the book and placed the drawings on the nearby nightstand, then slipped Eli's comforter over his shoulders. Pulling down the bedroom window shade, she paused to admire the countless stars shining in the night sky outside, blazing against the jet-black backdrop like millions of candles on an oversized birthday cake, then walked toward the door and flipped off the light.

As the room faded to black, Eli turned over and quietly mumbled, "Night, Mom."

"Sweet dreams, Eli," she responded.

Unfortunately, that would not be the case. Eli tossed and turned, finally lapsing into a dream. He watched in amazement as a dazzling white ghost who looked like his father slipped into his room through the polished chrome keyhole of the closed door. Eli saw him floating about a foot above the floor in a vaporlike state.

"Dad! What are you doing here?" Eli said.

With a curling index finger, the smiling phantom beckoned Eli to follow him.

Rubbing his eyes, Eli dutifully got out of bed. By now the ghost had left the bedroom and was floating down the corridor at a rapid pace. Eli followed, but the harder he tried to close ground between them, the farther away his father seemed to get. The two kept up their pursuit down a seemingly endless tunnel of rooms and doors.

Finally Eli started closing in, and he decided to fully commit to catching the ghost. Jumping head first toward it, he grasped at the floating white vapor. But just as his outstretched arms went through the apparition and grabbed at the material, the ghost completely vanished.

Eli crashed down hard on the hardwood floor, then woke up in a cold sweat. Puzzling over his nocturnal vision, he felt like a storm chaser trying to catch a twirling tornado. He knew one thing for certain: it was going to be a long night.

In the morning, light poured into Eli's bedroom through the opening of his partially drawn curtains. His mom came in with a bundle of perfectly folded white clothes. She nudged Eli, who was buried in a pile of pillows, and placed the bundle on the corner of his bed.

"Eli, time to wake up. You have a big baseball game this morning."

Chapter 5

Little League

Playing Little League baseball was a rite of passage for the kids in Eli's school, and Eli was no exception. But he had said he'd play only if he could be on the same team as Murph. This proved to be a good strategy, as Murph was the dominant player in the league.

Earl's dad, Gene, was the coach of the team—when he wasn't making flights to Japan for his job as an airline pilot—but he looked more like a nightclub bouncer. He was six-foot-four, with red hair and a matching bushy mustache. His booming laugh and easy smile put the players at ease in the dugout.

Earl and his dad proved the old adage "Like father, like son." Both had a propensity for hitting home runs: Gene smacked them over the fence in the local Parks and Recreation softball league, and Murph slammed them out of the park in Little League. Gene's favorite baseball player was "Big Daddy" Cecil Fielder, who played for the Detroit

43

Tigers back in the 1990s. Murph's hero was Prince Fielder, Cecil's son, who played for the same team today.

Eli, on the other hand, had never really enjoyed organized sports. He was reluctantly playing baseball because his parents thought it was a good idea for him to get out of the house and be part of a team.

Coach Gene had placed Eli in the barren wasteland of the baseball diamond: right field. Nothing interesting usually happened there, which was just the way Eli liked it. It gave him plenty of time to let his mind wander. Some kids passed their time in right field by picking dandelions, but Eli had more important things to do.

Today he was thinking about what his mom had said: "How about a car that can actually fly?" Her words echoed in his mind like a yodel in the Alps. "But how?" he said out loud. "Is it possible?"

Eli remembered a summer vacation a couple of years before, when his dad had taken him to Seattle over Labor Day weekend. It was a drizzly Saturday afternoon in the

Emerald City, so they'd decided to visit the Museum of Flight.

Eli had loved everything he saw there, but the most captivating thing was the Taylor Aerocar III—a prototype completed in 1949, but not certified by the Civil Aeronautics Administration until 1956. The car could transform itself into an airplane in five minutes.

Eli had marveled at the motorized mechanism. Now he started to wonder. What would happen if a car could *instantly* change into a plane?

Just then, Eli was snapped out of his daydream by a thunderous *ping* from an aluminum baseball bat behind home plate. The ball had shot off the bat like a meteor and was headed directly for him. It hung in the air for what seemed like an eternity, which gave him an opportunity to collect himself.

Other players were running toward the outfield, hoping Eli would catch the ball. At the last minute Eli dove backward and miraculously found the ball in the top webbing of his mitt.

The impact knocked the wind out of him. He could barely breathe. He was just relieved that he hadn't messed up the game for his team.

Murph ran to greet his best friend. "Way to go, Gold Glove!"

"What do you mean?" Eli asked. He was so uninterested in baseball, he didn't even know the lingo.

"Your fielding percentage is perfect on the season."

"That's because this is the first play I've made all season."

"Exactly," Murph chuckled as they jogged in unison back toward the dugout. "Hey, you made what they call a 'snow cone catch.' See, the ball is wedged in the top part of your glove like a single scoop in a cone."

In the final inning, Eli was up to bat. He managed to complete his specialty at the plate, a walk, and quickly jogged to first base as if he'd just won the lottery. The next two batters struck out, which left Murph to save the day. He jumped all over a high fastball and pounded it over a 225-foot fence in left field for his twenty-fifth home run of the season. The final score was 2-0 for their team.

After the game, the boys went out for ice cream. "What were you thinking about out in right field?" Murph asked.

"Not much," Eli said.

"Come on, I know that look. Did you think up anything good?"

"Maybe … I'm not sure," Eli said.

"Okay, okay … I get it. You don't want to talk about it. Whatever *it* is." Murph was starting to put two and two together.

"Hey, I'll give you a call later, okay?" Eli said.

"Sounds good. Catch you later. Get it, get it!" Murph reenacted Eli's backpedaling to catch the pop fly. The two boys smacked gloves as they walked out the door.

Chapter 6

Family Tree

On Saturday afternoon, Eli once again made his way to the old barn out back. It seemed to have a magnetic pull on him these days. Eli couldn't quite explain it, but he wanted to see the 1984 Martin Mercurio again.

He was pleased to see Grady near the barn. He was taking a break from cutting the grass on the riding lawn mower.

"Been thinking all morning about that trick you pulled off, catching that poor defenseless fish," Grady joked.

"That was no trick, Grady—that was an invention at its finest," Eli replied confidently.

"Guess you're right."

"Hey, do you know where the key is to my dad's car?" Eli asked sheepishly.

"I wouldn't do that if I were you," Grady warned.

"I'm not going to drive it. I just want to see a certain feature. Honest," Eli pleaded.

"Scout's honor?"

"Promise." Eli held up his fingers to make a Boy Scout salute.

Grady whisked some golden-colored hay off the barn floor to reveal a trapdoor. He lifted the rusty latch and tugged. The door finally relented after a few squeaks.

Grady reached down and carefully pulled up a slate gray plastic fishing-tackle box. He flipped its tarnished brass levers to open it, then removed an oversized worn silver car key. But it wasn't just any key. This was the magical key that would open the door to Eli's dad's first and favorite car.

Next they approached the car. After lifting off its dusty cover, they gently laid it on a nearby workbench. Eli put the key in the driver's-side door and turned it clockwise, holding his breath. The door opened, and Eli smoothly slid into the black leather seat.

For the second time in two days, Eli grasped the leather steering wheel. He felt like a trapeze artist reaching out for the swinging bar during a circus performance. Then his clammy hands pushed the key into the ignition, just far enough to hear a click. Rotating the key forward ever so slightly caused the dashboard to come to life. The needle measuring the amount of gas spiked up to full, and green lights flashed on, signaling that the Mercurio was ready and willing to move after all these years in hibernation. Bells chimed, letting Eli know that this sports car still had something left to prove. He could hardly contain his excitement.

Eli knew that if either his mom or his dad ventured down into the barn at this exact moment, he would be grounded for the rest of spring break. But he didn't care. This was just too good an opportunity to pass up.

Eli's curiosity spread to the car's accessories. He was particularly interested in the automatic seatbelt feature: whenever a passenger in the Mercurio closed the car door, the seatbelt would instantly slide into the correct locking position on the passenger's shoulders. Transfixed, Eli repeated the automated maneuver multiple times, carefully watching how the belt kept moving efficiently along the tracking mechanism by the edge of the window. His eyes blinked as if he were a spy camera recording classified documents on a secret mission.

Then, just as quickly as he had gotten into the car, he turned off the ignition, pulled out the key, and flipped it back to Grady for safekeeping.

"What are you thinking about, son?" Grady asked. He wasn't sure what this was all about.

But Eli had snapped back to reality. "Grady, what did you want to be when you were a kid?"

"That was a long time ago, Eli." Grady glanced out the window.

"I've got time. It is spring break, you know." Eli got out of the car, shut the door, and sat down on a nearby stool.

"Be careful what you ask for, Junior." Grady smirked at the ten-year-old.

"Go ahead. Dinner isn't for another hour." Eli settled in.

"Good, because this story could take a while," Grady said. "My grandfather, Grady Clarence Johnson the First, worked at the old Packard plant in downtown Detroit for over thirty years. The plant opened in 1907 and was considered a state-of-the-art car manufacturing facility."

"What does state-of-the-art mean, Grady?" Eli asked.

"It means the best of its kind. There were no finer cars than Packards," Grady said. "During the plant's heyday, it employed forty thousand skilled workers on a campus that spanned thirty-five acres. My grandpa was one of them. He thought life couldn't get much better than that."

"Forty thousand! That's a lot of people," Eli said.

"I know. Well, the fairy tale came crashing down in 1956, when the plant stopped manufacturing luxury sedans. Lickety-split, my grandpa was handed his walking papers." Grady paused for effect.

"What happened to the plant?" Eli inquired.

"Today it's abandoned. About the only people who go there are graffiti artists, industrial paint-ballers, and scrappers."

"What's a scrapper?"

"Scrappers are like the pirates of the city. They'll pull anything valuable off a building—copper pipes, electrical wire, fuse boxes, anything they can get their hands on—to turn around and sell for a couple of bucks."

"Oh. That sounds kind of fun," Eli said. "But sorry for the detour. Back to your story."

"Well, my grandpa was running out of his unemployment benefits when he received a phone call from your great-grandfather asking him to come work for Martin Motors. All the men in our family have been company men ever since."

"What's a company man?"

"Someone who works for the same company for his whole life."

"Did you follow in the family footsteps?" Eli asked.

"Certainly did. I worked Martin Motors assembly line number one, first shift, for over thirty years," Grady announced proudly.

"Did you ever want to do anything else?"

Grady hesitated. "I've never told anyone else this story, so I'm trusting you to keep it between the two of us, understand?"

Eli nodded, and Grady continued.

"When I was a little kid I wanted to be an astronaut. Man, I loved everything about NASA. The crisp white spacesuits, the whole mission to the moon, I even drank Tang. I'd beg my mom to put some Tang in my stocking for Christmas, and it would usually last until my birthday, when I'd ask for some more."

"What's Tang?" Eli asked.

"Tang is old-school Sunny D, you dig?" Grady responded.

"Got it, go on," Eli said.

"I did pretty well in school, so my teachers encouraged me to apply to George Washington Carver Technical High School. It was a magnet high school in math and science. Best high school in the city. Carver Tech was a lottery, and my ticket was punched.

"That sounds cool," Eli said.

"It was," Grady said. "I made good on my opportunity and did pretty well in school, son. Come senior year, I was top in my class and had already accepted a full-ride academic scholarship to the University of Michigan in the fall. I was living large and in charge. But then fate struck again."

"What happened?" Eli was riveted by the story.

"Well, you see, my dad loved bacon." Grady chuckled under his breath. "My pop ate bacon almost every meal. Bacon and eggs for breakfast, BLTs for lunch, and bacon cheeseburgers every Friday night for dinner. Man oh man, my dad sure loved his bacon.

"I like bacon too," Eli said hesitantly.

"Come Tuesday the week of my high school graduation, Dad was working the morning shift as usual, doing his job of assembling the bumpers to the chassis, when he commented to a coworker that he wasn't feeling too well. But he kept attaching his two hundred bumpers to the chassis just like on every other shift. Then he punched his time card, picked up his lunch pail from his locker—and dropped dead on the spot."

Eli was stunned. He stayed quiet for a minute, wondering if this could ever happen to his own father. He worked so hard. "What did you do?"

"Do? Well, I gave my class valedictorian commencement address on a Friday evening, buried my father on Saturday afternoon, and began working at Martin Motors on Monday morning. I never looked back."

"Why? I thought you wanted to be an astronaut," Eli said.

"I did want to be an astronaut, but there was my mom and my two baby sisters to look after, so it was time for me to be the man of the house. You can probably fill in the blanks of how the story ends. I picked up right where my father left off," Grady said proudly.

"Didn't you feel cheated on your dream?"

"The past is a nice place to visit, kid, but I wouldn't want to live there."

Eli looked dismayed.

"Hey, little man, it wasn't all bad," Grady said. "Your grandpa heard the story about my father and hired me first thing Monday morning. He even gave me the same shift my dad had, which I thought was pretty generous, considering I didn't have any seniority with the United Auto Workers."

"What's the United Auto Workers?" Eli asked.

"A union. It's a group that helps employees make their working conditions better and helps negotiate contracts with their employers, so they get a fair deal."

"How about your dad?" Eli asked wistfully. "Did you have a good relationship with your father?"

"Okay, I guess. My dad wasn't much of a talker, but my oh my, he sure loved his Detroit sports teams. Lions, Tigers, Pistons, you name it—he'd watch them all on the television. I wasn't that big into watching games myself, so I guess that made us have to search a little harder to find common ground, know what I mean?" Grady looked up and locked eyes with Eli.

"I do," Eli nodded knowingly. "What was your favorite part of your job?"

"About ten years into my career, your father started working at the company as a summer intern, as a way to learn the family business. He was just in his twenties then. Like you, he was a pretty sharp cookie, and curious as well."

"That was before I was born," Eli said.

"Oh yes," Grady said. "One day your dad came down to the assembly line on his lunch break and started asking folks what kind of cars Martin Motors should be making. All the other employees were hemming and hawing, not saying much. I guess they were kind of nervous and didn't want to seem to be pushing back on the boss."

"That was so nice of him to ask the workers what they thought," Eli said.

"Your dad was just about to leave when I bolstered up the courage to say one word: minivan," Grady said. "It was a concept I'd been thinking about for a while. And it must have caught your father's attention, because he turned around and quickly asked, 'Who said that?'"

"Wow, I can't believe you had the guts to speak up!" Eli said.

"I said, 'I did, sir.' I tipped my hard hat high on my forehead so he could get a good look at my face. He asked me what a minivan was. They're everywhere now, but this was before anyone had had the idea."

"How did you come up with it?" Eli asked.

"I'd been working at Martin Motors on assembly line number one for going on ten years. In the 1970s, we made one of the best station wagons around, but it had gone out of style. You know, styles change, and people's tastes are selective. But there's one thing that's certain." Grady paused dramatically.

"What's that?" Eli asked.

"People are going to have families. Some of them will have quite large ones. And these families are going to need to move from point A to point B. I told your dad all that. He seemed impressed and took me aside so we could talk further."

"What did you say?" Eli asked.

"I told him that station wagons were out of style, and people found industrial vans too large and cumbersome to drive, so why not make an automobile that was a cross between the two? I called it a minivan," Grady said. "He liked

60

the idea and said he'd bounce it off his dad, who ran the company."

"And?" Eli asked.

"Two years later, Martin Motors came out with the first minivan of any kind and sold more than 300,000 units in the first year of production. Of course, all the other car companies jumped into that space as well, but it was still seen as a pioneering achievement: building an all-new make and model of vehicle out of thin air. From vapor to minivan," Grady proudly announced.

"Did you get anything out of it?" Eli was remembering what he'd learned in Monopoly about business.

"I did get naming rights for the term 'minivan,' which helped get my sisters through college, but I didn't break the bank, if you know what I mean," Grady said.

Eli nodded his head in an understanding way. Then he blurted out the first thought that popped into his mind, even though it wasn't about minivans. "I rarely get to see my dad. He's like a ghost that floats in and out of my life, but I never really feel like I can grab his attention and get hold of him."

"I know what you mean, son…. I really do. My father was often in the same room as me, but I always wondered if he was really there for me. You know, did he have my back?"

"I guess that's why I wanted to sit in his car," Eli said. "I thought maybe I'd feel just a little bit closer to him somehow."

"Well, do you, Junior?" Grady asked.

"Do I what?"

"Feel any closer to your father."

"I'm not sure. It's complicated," Eli said.

Their fine Saturday afternoon was fading to dusk, which meant that Eli needed to run back to the house for dinner. Grady opened his worn palm, crisscrossed with lines of age, and inspected the silver car key. Then he slid it back into the old metal tackle box, flipped the brass latches closed, and nestled it in its hiding place. Finally, he slowly dropped the wooden hatch down level with the barn floor

and slid some loose straw back over the top.

The location of the key to the special car from Eli's

dad's youth was once again a well-kept secret.

Chapter 7

Sunday

Sunday was the one day of the week when Eli could count on having some quality time with his dad. After church, the Martins would usually head over to brunch at the local country club.

Eli loved having the opportunity to get caught up with his father. On this particular Sunday, he told his dad all about the big baseball contest the day before, including the highlight: making the game-saving catch and scoring the tying run when Murph smacked the baseball over the fence for a two-run, game-winning homer.

Then he asked his dad about something he'd been reading about. "What do you know about jet packs, Dad?"

"You mean jet propulsion?" Dad asked.

"You got it."

"When I was around your age, I loved to read comic books," Dad said. "My favorite was called *The Rocketeer*, and its hero was named Cliff Secord. He was an ace pilot who goes on to become a rocketeer who uses a jet pack. I spent a lot of time sitting on my bed thinking about jet packs."

"Really?" Eli said. Learning that his dad was interested in the same thing he was always made him feel good.

"I was so sure that jet-pack technology would be ready and available for commercial use by the twenty-first century," Dad said. "But there have been some pretty significant setbacks."

"Like what?"

"First off, they can stay airborne for only about thirty seconds. Second, the hydrogen peroxide propellant is pretty expensive, and third, the human body is not adapted to fly naturally."

"But what if man could fly? Imagine the possibilities!" Eli said.

"No more rush-hour traffic," Dad said.

"Or going through security at the airport," Eli countered.

"No more busy soccer moms commuting to the park," Mom interjected.

"Well, it is fun to dream. Check, please." Dad concluded the conversation and brunch with one efficient gesture.

Back home, Eli settled in to play a game of Trivial Pursuit with his mom and dad. The irony of this family tradition was that Eli consistently won the game, in which players had to answer players' questions in categories such as People and Places, History, Science and Nature, Entertainment, Sports and Leisure, and Wild Card.

He was strategically positioned smack dab in the middle of the board, and on his usual winning streak, when his mom read the final question: "Who coined the phrase 'Insanity is doing the same thing over and over again, but expecting a different result'?"

A smile spread across Eli's lips as he correctly answered the question—"Albert Einstein"—thus winning the game. His parents shook his hand, congratulating the champion. Then his dad got a serious look on his face.

"Question for you, son. How come you know most of the answers to these questions, but are not doing well in Mrs. Fitzgerald's class?" he asked.

"Bored, I guess," Eli mumbled.

Mom chimed in. "I've heard that people don't learn from teachers they don't like. Is it Mrs. Fitzgerald?"

"I like Mrs. F. She's great," Eli said dismissively.

"What is it, Eli? You can tell us," Mom said reassuringly.

Dad chimed in. "What your mother's trying to say is that we know you're a bright boy—we'd like to see what you're capable of."

"Isn't winning Trivial Pursuit every week enough?"

"Son, playing Trivial Pursuit is not on your report card. If it was, you'd be on the dean's list." Dad reached over and ruffled Eli's hair.

"Dad, do you know what it's like to be called the Noah Tall of class?"

"Sorry, I'm not following you."

"The kids in class started calling me Noah Tall in third grade. Noah Tall, know-it-all. They thought I was sucking up to the teachers by knowing all the answers to their questions. After a while, I just stopped volunteering in class because I knew I'd be made fun of at recess."

"Sounds rough. Can you humor the old man and at least pretend to pay attention in class?"

"Okay, okay … I'll try."

"That's all we're asking," Mom said.

"I have one last trivia question for you, Dad. Who played the Incredible Invisible Man in the 2012 remake of the famous original movie?"

"I don't know, who?" Dad shrugged his shoulders.

Eli looked his dad squarely in the eyes and said, "Michael Martin."

"Hey, that's not exactly fair, Eli!" Dad said.

"Oh yeah? Why don't you take a good look at the drawing of our family that I made when I was seven?" Eli said. "It's still on the refrigerator."

Eli's dad walked to the kitchen and spotted his son's drawing. It had worked its way down the fridge door by now, but was still there. He vaguely remembered seeing it when Eli had brought it home a few years ago, but hadn't looked at it since. He was always so rushed when he was at home.

"What do you notice?" Eli asked.

His dad looked closely at the Crayola stick figures in the drawing. He could clearly identify Eli and his mom, who were holding hands and smiling. Right next to them was a crude charcoal gray skyscraper. On top of the building, sitting in an office chair, was a daddy stick figure.

His dad didn't need any interpretation to grasp the meaning. He already felt guilty enough for having been an absentee father lately. He took off his glasses and rubbed his eyes.

Satisfied at having made his point, Eli slid his dining room chair across the hardwood floor and headed upstairs to his room without looking back. He snatched his sketchbook off his nightstand and started to draw.

Pictures sprang to life on the pages of his book—fanciful, wonderful images, like a car with doors that could pivot around the perimeter of a door casing, and doors that locked into position like the wings of a small airplane.

One especially detailed sketch showed what would happen after the car's doors extended like wings. As Eli imagined it, thin windows made of something like Plexiglas would slide down and cover the vacant door openings. The windows would create a sealed-up cockpit within the confines of the car, which would help combat the effects of atmospheric pressure and wind currents.

Eli sat back on his bed and smiled at his latest burst of imagination. A single thought was beginning to make its way into his mind: could he possibly bring his vision to life?

Chapter 8

Just Another Manic Monday

Eli woke up on Monday morning with a new sense of purpose. "How old was Mark Zuckerberg when he created Facebook?" he asked himself.

But he already knew the answer—just twenty years old. As Eli's dad always said, "Just because you're young doesn't mean you can't achieve greatness."

Eli revived his senses by splashing his face with cold water, then threw on his favorite yellow and blue University of Michigan hoodie and hopped into a worn pair of blue jeans he found crumpled in a corner of the room next to his laundry basket. He knew exactly where he needed to go: back to his laboratory.

Most people wouldn't have pegged the big old barn out back as a science lab, but Eli recognized that it was a place where invention intersected with inspiration. If his great-grandfather had created the very first Martin Motors vehicle in this same spot, it was only to be expected that history would repeat itself.

Eli snatched his sketchbook and sprinted down to the barn, thinking of the endless possibilities. Once more he grabbed the iron key from underneath the wooden rooster, opened the double doors to the barn, and went over to look at the Martin Mercurio. He had one goal: to figure out whether his two-dimensional drawings could become a three-dimensional reality.

Just then, there was a rustling outside. Grady pulled one of the barn doors open and popped his head in. "Thought I might find you in here."

"What do you know about jet propulsion?" Eli blurted out.

"A little," Grady replied, scratching his stubbly white beard.

"Come on, you were supposed to be an astronaut. Can't you do better than that?"

"The necessary velocity required to escape Earth's orbit is 11.2 kilometers per second. How's that, Mr. Smartypants?"

"I don't need to escape Earth's orbit. In fact, quite the opposite. I want to stay in the Earth's atmosphere."

"Boy, you are talking nonsense."

"Actually, it makes perfect sense. You're just not thinking big enough."

"What are you proposing, son?" Grady asked, looking thoughtful.

"Are you thinking what I'm thinking?"

"I'm thinking I'm getting too old for this." Grady took out his red handkerchief and wiped his brow.

"That's probably true, but you're all I've got." Eli nudged Grady playfully.

"You're all I *have*," Grady corrected him. "Now, what exactly are you planning to do?"

"*We*, as in you and me, are going to build a car that flies."

"How do you suppose *we're* going to do that?"

"We'll start with this." Eli patted the hood of the Martin Mercurio.

"Last time I checked, that car didn't have a Chitty Chitty Bang Bang button," Grady joked.

"What's that?" Eli asked.

"*Chitty Chitty Bang Bang* was an old movie about a car that flies, Junior."

"Let me show you something." Eli opened his sketchbook of blueprints.

"These are good, son, real good," Grady said, paging through the book. "You drew these yourself?"

"Yep."

"Mmm, mmm, mmm … this just might work."

"I think it can," Eli said.

"Why do you want to make a car that flies, son?"

"I never get to see my dad. Well, not exactly never, but only on Sundays," Eli said. "He always has some lame excuse—'Busy day at work, son,' or 'The traffic was a killer today, Eli.'"

"Sorry to hear that," Grady said.

"If I could make a car that actually flies," Eli said, "then maybe, just maybe, I might get to see my dad more often."

Grady thought back to his own memories of his dad. He felt sad that history was repeating itself with Eli and his father.

"I've calculated how much time my dad could save on his commute time if he could fly to and from work every day," Eli said. "He'd save forty minutes a day. Multiply that times five days in a typical workweek, and that's two hundred minutes in the first week alone. Now multiply two hundred minutes a week by fifty weeks a year, and we're up to ten thousand minutes saved annually—roughly 167 hours of his life that my dad would get back each year by commuting in a flying car."

"Hmm, hmm, hmm," Grady said. "What would you call a car like that?"

"I'd keep it simple," Eli said. "Call it Fly Car."

"Okay, kid," Grady said. "If we're going to give this a try, then you have to do your homework, got it? I want you to read as much as you can about wings, and not just the basics. You'll have to know about more than just drag and lift. I'll start getting the specifics on the 1984 Martin Mercurio—total weight, zero to sixty times, engine capacity—and we'll meet back here at lunchtime."

Eli sat open-mouthed. Were they really going to do this? He hadn't thought it would be so easy to persuade Grady.

"Well, don't just sit there—get cracking, son!"

Eli didn't need to be told twice. He peeled out of the barn's double doors and sprinted up to the main house, excited about possibly making history—or at least getting a few more minutes a day with his dad. Up in his room, he eagerly opened at his laptop and began searching the Internet for information on how planes fly.

Eli had always marveled at how a machine as massive as a plane could actually get off the ground as it accelerated down the runway for takeoff. As he researched the mechanics of lift, he started to understand how the process worked. The force occurs when a solid object deflects a moving fluid. The wing splits the airflow in two directions: up and over the wing, and down along the underside of the wing.

The wing is shaped and tilted so that the air moving over it travels faster than the air moving underneath. When moving air flows over an object and encounters an obstacle, such as a bump or a sudden increase in wing angle, its path narrows and the flow speeds up as all the molecules rush though. Once past the obstacle, the path widens and the flow slows again.

It's like when a water hose is pinched, Eli realized. The path of the water flow is narrowed, which speeds up the molecules. When you remove the pressure, the water flow returns to its previous state. That's why, in a water fight, you always put a thumb over the opening of the hose to get the liquid to spray with more force and greater distance.

As air speeds up, its pressure drops. So the faster-moving air moving over the wing exerts less pressure on it than the slower air moving underneath the wing. The result is an upward push of lift. In the field of fluid dynamics, Eli learned, this is known as Bernoulli's principle. He loved the sound of it.

If the maximum weight of a Boeing 747 is 900,000 pounds, or roughly 450 tons, Eli reasoned, and a 747 routinely gets up in the air and carries four or five hundred passengers to their destination, surely he could get Fly Car to do the same with much less weight and only a few passengers.

His brain ached as he pondered the possibilities. He now had a better idea of how the wings would need to be configured, but each answer gave way to more questions. How would the car seamlessly convert to a plane? How long should the wings be? What amount of thrust would be needed to get Fly Car off the ground?

There were no easy answers, Eli knew. Each possibility would need to be researched and tried, and some would likely fail. He might even end up going back to the drawing board entirely.

Eli went down to the barn once more on this blustery mid-April afternoon. Massive cumulus clouds marched across the sky like a herd of elephants looking for a watering hole. Eli shared some of his findings with Grady and compared notes. Then Grady brought out a kite from the old barn.

"What's that for?" Eli asked.

"You'll see soon enough," Grady said.

The two traipsed out onto the vast lawn to gauge the direction of the wind. It was blowing steadily from a northwesterly direction.

Grady held the kite and gave the ball of string to Eli. "You better start running, son."

Eli took off as fast as his skinny legs could carry him. The kite was soon soaring in the patchy blue sky.

Grady and Eli both started smiling. Even though they weren't on the level of Ben Franklin and his son William, who had used a kite to discover electricity, they'd still found out something important.

"What did you learn from this little experiment, Eli?" Grady asked.

"Weight's opposing force is lift, which holds an airplane in the air," Eli said. "Lift is accomplished through the use of a wing, also known as an airfoil. Like drag, lift can exist only in the presence of a moving fluid. It doesn't matter if the object is stationary and the fluid is moving, as with this kite up in the sky on a windy day, or if the fluid is still and the object is moving through it, as with a soaring jet on a windless day. What really matters is the relative difference in speeds between the object and the fluid."

"You've been doing your homework." Grady grinned. "What else?"

Just then Eli had a Eureka moment, and he looked at Grady curiously. How come no teacher at Thomas Edison Elementary had ever gotten him to think like this before? "I'm thinking the lawn will serve as a great runway for takeoffs and landings."

"Bingo!" Grady said. "It's perfect: long, flat, and immaculately mowed, if I do say so myself. We'll start on this project tomorrow."

Eli allowed the kite to slowly pitch from side to side as it returned to the ground. Rolling up the string, he began dreaming about a vehicle that would one day take off and land within the confines of Martin Manor.

Chapter 9

I'd Like Some Wings, Please

Eli knew that figuring out the mass and configuration of Fly Car's wings was going to be a Herculean challenge. They'd need to be lightweight yet tough enough to resist any puncture or changing wind currents.

What lightweight metal was plentiful and inexpensive? The only substance Eli could think of was aluminum. He could collect aluminum cans from the neighbors, then melt them and reshape the metal to create aerodynamic winglike extensions of the car's doors.

As soon as he'd answered that question, more popped to mind. Where could the wings be hidden when Fly Car was just a car driving down the road? How would they rotate and lock into place? When they were extended, what would replace the empty void where the doors had been? The answers were elusive, but after careful thought and consideration, they too waltzed into his mind.

Eli and Grady started meeting up every day after school to work on the project. Grady liked the drawings of the wings that Eli had created during his late-night hours with his sketchbook. The question was how to make them come alive.

Eli and Grady decided to make a balsa-wood model of the wings first. Making a three-dimensional mockup would help them work the kinks out of their design, and balsa wood was an inexpensive material to work with. They were so motivated that within a few days, they had completed a workable pair of balsa-wood wings.

Meanwhile, over the next few weeks, Eli collected over a thousand aluminum cans, going door to door and asking neighbors if they could contribute their used recyclables. He'd stealthily drag the bags of cans back into the barn every night, when he took out the trash—one of the chores around the house that he did to earn his allowance.

Eli even paid Murph $50 for the aluminum-can collection he'd been amassing for some time. Murph briefly wondered where Eli came up with that kind of cash, but then he remembered that Eli was always squirreling away his allowance money in secret compartments around his room. He was mildly curious about Eli's sudden need for aluminum, but knew he was always inventing something.

As the number of aluminum cans in the barn mounted, Grady got even more excited about the project. One day he brought in an old blowtorch to show Eli. "This is from my days of working on the Martin Motors assembly line."

"Great! You can use that to melt the aluminum," Eli said. "Did you know that aluminum has a melting point of roughly 1,221 degrees Fahrenheit?"

"Yes, and I know something else: that temperature is a palindrome, Junior," Grady said.

"What's a palindrome?"

"A word—or, in this case, a number—that reads the same both forward and backward."

"You're pretty smart, aren't you, Grady?"

"Mmm, mmm, mmm, son."

Grady patiently heated up and melted the cans, using the blowtorch as a modified forge. Then he placed the silvery liquid metal in molds. From there, he carefully stretched the metal into aluminum sheets that looked like enormous pieces of tin foil, but much thicker. They were roughly five millimeters thick, in fact—the same as a commercial aircraft skin.

The aluminum sheets turned out better than expected, but Grady and Eli also discovered a problem: even with so many cans, they had only enough aluminum to make one wing.

Eli went back to pounding the pavement, collecting a thousand more cans, this time with Murph's help. They had to scour a nearby neighborhood this time, so as not to draw too much attention to the project. Eli offered Murph another $50 for helping him gather the all-important scrap metal.

"Okay, but on one condition—you tell me what's up," Murph said. "What's with all the aluminum?"

Eli wanted to tell Murph about Fly Car, but he was afraid his buddy would blab the details of his invention to the entire fifth grade. He blushed and blurted out the first words that came to his mind.

"Science experiment," he said.

Murph started jumping up and down like an overgrown golden retriever puppy. "Can I see it?"

"Not exactly. I mean, it's not quite finished yet. But I promise you'll be the first one to get a look once it's completed." Eli hoped this would be enough to satisfy Murph for now.

"Okay," Murph said. "Say, did I ever tell you about the time I pushed a vitamin up my nose and the pill got stuck? A few days later, I had to go to the doctor and have it removed when my mom noticed an enormous hump on the side of my right nostril."

Eli laughed. He liked that Murph didn't pry too much. Also, he was easily distracted.

"Hey, do you want to go in the hot tub?" Eli asked. He loved soaking in the big octagonal hot tub behind the house, just off the corner of the deck.

"Sure!" Murph said. He was always game for a relaxing soak.

Eli entered gingerly, walking slowly down the steps into the hot tub so as not to slip. Murph meanwhile, chose to cannonball directly into the water.

When Murph came up for air, Eli asked him a pointed question. "Murph, what's it like when your dad pilots an international flight with a layover, so he's gone for a long time?"

"You can hear the crickets at home," Murph replied solemnly.

"Why do you think that is?"

"I guess because everyone misses him. But it comes out in funny ways."

"What do you mean?"

"My dad's kind of like an overgrown kid. He has a way of lightening up a situation."

"Yeah, my dad has a calming effect at home as well. When he's around." Eli was quiet for a minute. "What do you like to do with your dad?"

"Play catch in the backyard." Murph said.

"Why?"

"It's a chance to talk to him and get caught up, especially after he's been gone for a while," Murph said. "How about you? What do you like to do with your dad?"

"Fishing." Eli looked up and smiled.

"Fishing is boring," Murph responded in a matter-of-fact tone.

"That's exactly why I love it. It's one of the few times when I have all of his attention," Eli said. "When we're out on Old Man Murphy's Pond, there are no gadgets, no distractions—it's simple, peaceful even. I can talk to my father about almost anything when we're in the boat."

"That does sound cool," Murph said.

"Dad doesn't even bring his smart phone," Eli said. "He says it distracts the fish, but I think he really does it for me, so we can just talk."

Just then, Eli's mom slid open the screen door. "Murph, time to go home! Your family's about to have dinner."

89

The boys hopped out of the hot tub and dried themselves with colorful beach towels. It was a beautiful evening. A pink hue filled the sky as a robin chirped a tune in a neighboring white pine.

"See you tomorrow, Murph," Eli said, sliding the screen door open and heading into his own house. His mouth watered as he smelled the barbecued chicken on the grill inside.

Chapter 10

Houston, We Have a Problem

Grady continued to work on the wings for Fly Car in his spare time, melting the aluminum cans, placing the cooling liquid in molds, and stretching it into sheets. Meanwhile, he was pondering how to get a pair of extensions to attach to the inverted door panels to actually create the wings.

Eli and Grady had already figured out how the doors would need to maneuver forward over the front wheel well by using a track sliding mechanism, much like the one used for the doors of minivans. The doors would then shift back toward the main frame in a parallel motion to the chassis of the car and tightly lock into place.

The door on either side would serve as the base of the two wings on the converted craft. From there, a thin sheet of Plexiglas would quickly descend downward from the top to make Fly Car's interior a fully functioning airtight cockpit.

Getting the doors to shift and lock into place was relatively easy, but making the wings aerodynamic was a challenge. Grady reasoned that there would be some room between the inside armrest of each door and the metal exterior. He knew he'd have to clear some of the space in the hidden compartment to create enough area for the wing extensions, but it could be done.

Would the wing extensions actually fit, Grady wondered, and could they be expanded through the tip of the converted doors that now served as wings? After completing a little design research, he knew the answer to those questions.

A sliding device would need to be installed inside the car door that would allow the wing to expand and retract, Grady thought, like a drawbridge in the days of medieval castles and moats. It had to be functional and efficient at the same time. He began tinkering with the concept of levers and pulleys that could be connected to the window-opening mechanism, and that would allow the wing extension to connect to the end of the current car door base that was now serving as a wing.

After a while, though, Grady got tired of thinking so intensely. He decided to take a siesta during his lunch break to clear his mind. While napping, he dreamed of a solution: yo-yos.

He had a flashback to a vivid moment from his childhood. He was ten years old and mesmerized by a demonstration by that year's Duncan Yo-Yo champion, who was putting on a show at a downtown toy store a few days before Christmas. The show was aimed at boosting yo-yo sales during the holidays.

Grady remembered watching as the yo-yo master shot the string out from his wrist like Spider-Man releasing a web to capture a criminal. The first trick he taught the audience was the Sleeper, in which he sent the yo-yo whizzing down to barely an inch off the floor, spinning and hissing like a whirling top. At the last minute, he popped it back into his hand, much to the delight of the gathered shoppers.

Grady woke up inspired by the dream. Could it solve his current design dilemma? Unlike the yo-yo, Fly Car's wing extensions would have to move more like an elevator, with an up-and-down motion along a wire tether. He needed some sort of two-way pulley mechanism....

Suddenly the concept came to him: a garage door! On the sides of a garage door are two pulleys with hooks, which allow the wheels to move along a track system, automatically lifting the weight of the door. If he could create a smaller-scale pulley system, Grady reasoned, then the wings could extend to the end of the car doors on each side to create a relatively lightweight, aerodynamic wing. It just might work, he thought.

Curious to find out, Grady made his way down to the local hardware store. He purchased four pulleys—two for each side—and some three-quarter-inch reinforced twisted cable wire. He tossed the bag in the back of his old truck and headed back to Martin Manor. After creating a thirty-six-inch pulley system on each side of the door that fit snugly inside the hollowed-out compartment, Grady sealed the mechanism inside the panel.

Next it was time to test the wing extensions. Grady made sure the car doors were tightly shut, then pushed the cruise control button on the steering wheel, which he'd converted to control the wings. The doors rocked along the tracks, first moving forward to the front wheel well, and then sliding backward into place with a click.

He tapped the button a second time, then watched with increasing excitement as the wing extension moved into place, creating a pair of seven-foot aerodynamic wings on either side of the craft. "Perfect!" Grady exclaimed, and began doing a touchdown dance inside the otherwise still barn.

Eli rushed home from school that day, excited to tell his mom about his first day back after spring break. He'd also been wondering all day if Grady had made any progress on Fly Car.

Eli came bursting into the barn. "Hey, Grady, anything happen today?"

"I solved the wing issue!" Grady said proudly.

"Really? Can you give me a demonstration?"

"Get behind the wheel, kid."

Eli rubbed his sweaty palms on his faded blue jeans and hopped into the driver's seat. He listened carefully to Grady's instructions and hit the wing control button a single time. Suddenly the car doors transformed before his eyes. They started shifting along the tracking mechanism, preparing to extend into wings. Eli's heart began to race.

He counted to ten slowly and then pressed the wing control button once more. A pair of flaps opened from within each door, and the pulleys began moving the wings into place, extending the doors into a pair of seven-foot wings. Finally, a clear protective Plexiglas cover slid down, taking up the open space where the car doors had been.

Eli sat in awe. The car had made a complete metamorphosis into a plane—in less than a minute! The Taylor Aerocar III had taken far longer—five minutes—to convert from car to plane.

Eli began jumping up and down, then blurted out the first thought that came into his mind.

"We've got to give Fly Car a test drive—I mean, flight!"

"We don't even know if it can make it off the ground, son," Grady said,

"We'll never know unless we try. What did Thomas Edison say? 'I have not failed. I've just found ten thousand ways that won't work.'"

"Yeah, but we have only one Martin Mercurio, and it's your dad's most prized possession. What if we total it?"

"My great-grandfather rolled out the very first Martin motorized vehicle in this barn. He pioneered the family business right here. We're talking ground zero for Martin innovation. Where's your sense of adventure, Grady?" Eli said.

"Adventure is for young people, Eli. If you haven't noticed, I have a few more miles on the tires than you do."

"Listen, Grady, we could continue the legacy this very day," Eli said. "You may never have become an astronaut, but that doesn't mean you can't get a little closer to exploring the heavens."

"Okay, you got me, Junior. Let's do it," Grady said, smiling. "Here's another Edison quote you'll like: 'Heck, there are no rules here, we're just trying to accomplish something.'"

"Now that's the spirit!" Eli said.

Chapter 11

Trial and Error

Eli made it his daily ritual to bug Grady for a specific time and date to launch Fly Car. But as the days passed, Grady became more reluctant—or, maybe, realistic—about the prospects of Fly Car actually getting off the ground.

"Come on, Grady, what were you telling me a few months back about it being okay to fail—just fail fast and forward?" Eli pleaded.

"Yeah, but this is different. Our lives are at stake. Besides, what will your parents think?" Grady countered.

"My parents are going out of town this weekend to testify in Washington, D.C., about the state of the Big Three automakers," Eli said. "They tried to pawn me off to some high school babysitter, but I convinced them that you'd take better care of me." Eli smirked.

"I don't like the sound of this, Junior." Grady shook his head.

"I checked the meteorology reports, and the weather conditions are optimum for a test flight," Eli said. "Five-mile-an-hour winds from the north. So Saturday morning is go time." He was sure about Fly Car, even if Grady wasn't.

Grady finally relented. "Tomorrow it is."

Saturday morning came early. The cool spring air brought a chill to the skin and an alertness to the senses. Grady had Eli retract Fly Car's wings so it could comfortably fit through the barn's double doors. Early morning sunlight and blue skies kissed the barn floor, and the smell of old hay wafted through the open structure. The two hopeful inventors pushed the car carefully through the opening, much as a seasoned pit crew massages a NASCAR competitor back onto the racetrack.

Eli knew the vast lawn would provide more than enough space for an initial test flight. He and Grady threw on bike helmets before preparing for takeoff. Both pilot and passenger had so many unanswered questions racing through their minds. Would Fly Car actually ascend into the sky? How high would it go? Would they be able to successfully land the car craft?

Eli and Grady agreed not to tempt fate during the maiden flight. Five to ten minutes sounded about right. They also decided that Grady should be the one behind the steering wheel. He didn't have a pilot's license, but he had been the proud owner of a driver's license for over forty years, with no accidents or speeding violations.

As they taxied Fly Car down the middle of the manicured meadow, their hearts raced. Grady asked the boy one more time, "Are you sure you're up for this, son?" All he received in return was a single word of confirmation: "Absolutely." Grady pulled up on the emergency brake, pushed the gas pedal to the floor, and gripped the steering wheel tightly, as if it were the horn of a saddle on a mechanical bull.

At the edge of the property stood a series of interlocking black gum trees roughly seventy feet tall that formed a natural fence. Would Fly Car have enough speed to clear the trees, given a takeoff angle of fifteen degrees?

As the cherry red sports car barreled down the pathway, sweat started to form on Grady's furrowed brow. "Come on baby, clear," he whispered. Three hundred yards from the trees, Grady pulled back on the steering wheel and Fly Car started to ascend rapidly. It was gaining a steady altitude of ten feet every second.

Unfortunately, the black gum trees stood directly ahead. Fly Car scraped the tops of the twisted tree branches with an ear-piercing screech and began to descend rapidly as the unforgiving trees punctured massive holes in both aluminum wings.

There was little time to think—they had to quickly decide where to land the car. Grady decided to drop it into Old Man Murphy's Pond. He cranked the steering wheel firmly to his left and banked the plane toward the coffee-colored waters.

Fly Car slapped the surface of the overgrown pond, and water cascaded over the top like a tidal wave. Grady depressed the Plexiglas windows, and both passenger and pilot made a successful eleventh-hour evacuation. The car quickly sank fifteen feet down, coming to a rest on the bottom of the pond.

Eli swam and Grady dog-paddled over to the muddy banks of the shore. Sopping wet, but thankful to still be alive, the two inventors collapsed on a mossy knoll next to the nearby willow tree. They were spent from the stress of the crash landing and sudden evacuation. But after a few minutes, Eli gathered his senses and piped up.

"That was absolutely amazing!" he exclaimed. "We were actually flying! Can you believe it? In 1903, the Wright Brothers' total flight time was roughly twelve seconds. We were airborne for a minute and thirty seconds. Incredible!"

Catching his breath, Grady leaned up and stabilized himself with his arms. "Did I miss something here, or did we just total your dad's car?"

"Just a technicality," Eli replied.

Chapter 12

The Deep Dive

The soggy pair made their way back to the barn. "What do we do now?" Eli asked eagerly.

"Do?" Grady replied. "I'd better start packing my bags and looking for a new job, that's what *I* need to do. I should have never listened to you in the first place. I'm a goner for sure."

"You won't get fired," Eli assured the nervous groundskeeper. "Not if you don't get caught."

"How can we manage that?"

"We need to find a way to get Fly Car back up to the surface and detailed before my mom and dad get back from their trip to Washington, D.C. Got any ideas?"

"How are you going to pay to have the car completely vacuumed, waxed, and polished, Junior? Detailing costs a lot of money."

"Don't worry about the detailing details for now," Eli said. "First things first—how are we going to get Fly Car surfaced and back into the barn?"

"My uncle has a towing company," Grady said. "I could use his truck with a winch after hours. Let me give him a call."

Grady secured the towing rig for that very evening. He and Eli decided to lift the vehicle at night, when it was completely dark, to keep the neighbors from knowing about the untimely crash landing earlier in the day.

Grady had told Eli to meet him at the base of the old willow tree at 10:30 p.m., so Eli snuck out the back of Martin Manor at 10:15 p.m. The night was pitch black; fireflies dotted the grass like nature's fireworks show. The air was cool for mid-May, which made Eli zip up his hoodie.

Eli signaled his flashlight twice, and Grady responded by holding up three neon green scuba-diving glow sticks. A full moon reflected off the glassy surface of Old Man Murphy's Pond.

"So what's the game plan?" Eli asked.

"Well, since you're a better swimmer than I am," Grady said, "I thought you could swim out to the middle of the pond, dive down, and connect the towing hook to Fly Car's bumper."

"I was afraid you were going to say that." Eli flashed a nervous smile.

"Then I can try to pull the car out. Got it?"

"I guess so," Eli said.

"Come on, what are you waiting for? The night isn't getting any younger. Besides, I need to get the tow truck back to my uncle by tomorrow morning at the latest." Grady reached for the bag of snorkeling gear he'd brought with him.

Eli dutifully peeled off his clothes down to his surf shorts and swim shirt. Grady gave him the three glow sticks. Eli placed one in each hand and the third around his neck. He walked barefoot along the banks of the pond, looking for the best place to jump in. Mud oozed through his toes like raw chocolate chip cookie dough.

Finally, he reached a likely spot and stopped. Grady handed him a scuba mask, a pair of flippers, and a snorkel.

Eli cleaned his toes and the backs of his heels one at a time, trying to rinse most of the mud off his feet before putting on the rubber flippers. They fit comfortably, like Cinderella's glass slipper. From there, he adjusted the mask on his face to seal the fit.

At last Eli was fully equipped. He grabbed the twisted two-inch steel cable and towing hook and began wading in backward through the lily pads and elongated cattails toward the wreckage, until the water forced him to breast-stroke with his head up the rest of the way out into the middle of the pond.

Algae whisked across his legs like cobwebs in the dark corners of a haunted house. He shuddered and wondered if he could actually follow through with this mission. He gave himself a much-needed pep talk. "You can do this, Eli! You're almost there."

He was now roughly thirty yards out into the pond. Before diving downward, Eli looked back at Grady, who was standing on the bank with the tow truck backed up to the edge. Now came the worst part of the mission: descending to the murky depths to locate his dad's classic car.

Eli took in massive gulps of air, as he had once seen pearl divers do on a public television program, and took the plunge. As he descended, a largemouth bass suddenly popped into his field of vision and stared directly at him with its massive bulging eyes. The mask's magnification made the creature look three times larger than it actually was. Eli's heart thumped as he broke to the surface, abandoning his goal, frightened and gasping for air.

The glow sticks made the surface of the water appear radioactive. He began to wonder if he could go through with the dive.

But after taking in a few gulps of oxygen, he began to collect his thoughts. He remembered the tire experiment, in which he had captured a similar-looking fish. The thought calmed him enough to make another diving attempt.

Once again, Eli began accumulating as much air as possible in his lungs. When he was at maximum lung capacity, he made a quick 180-degree turn and began kicking his flippers vigorously. The movement propelled him rapidly down to the bottom of the pond.

He reached Fly Car in fifteen seconds. This gave him another thirty seconds to attach the towing hook to the back bumper. He looped the hook and steel cable firmly around the middle of the bumper, tied off the back, and, with his last bit of energy, gave the cable a firm tug. His lungs were on fire as he began the ascent back to the surface and safety.

Grady greeted him with a well-deserved dry towel.

"Your turn—time to raise Fly Car!" Eli said.

"Aye-aye, Captain," Grady joked. He cautiously brought in the winch and steel cable, which was threaded onto an oversized metal spool on the back of the tow truck. After five minutes, Fly Car breached the surface of Old Man Murphy's Pond like a humpback whale. Half an hour later, it was drained and safely back inside the barn. There would definitely be more work to do on the car, but Eli and Grady shook hands knowing they were back in business.

Chapter 13

The Resurrection

Eli's parents returned to Martin Manor early the next morning. His dad soon left for the office to get caught up on some paperwork.

Eli smiled at his mom and welcomed her home. "How lucky that this just happened to be Memorial Day weekend," he thought. "Now we have an extra day to repair Fly Car."

Grady and Eli met inside the barn at 8 a.m. Monday. Eli yawned broadly, still tired from last night's rescue mission. They both agreed that the car needed to be detailed. That way, it would at least have a consistent visual appearance both inside and out.

Eli had read somewhere that if a cell phone went through a washing machine by accident, it might still be salvaged if it was immediately packed in rice as a way of drying out the battery. Could the same method be used to dry out Fly Car's engine? He convinced Grady to take him to a local warehouse superstore, where he purchased four fifty-pound bags of rice and gently laid them around the sides of the car's engine.

On Tuesday after school, Eli raced home to see if his grand evaporation experiment had been successful. In the barn, he carefully removed the bags of rice from the car's engine and laid them next to a workbench in the corner. He was surprised by how much heavier they seemed, compared to the previous night. They'd clearly absorbed a fair amount of the pond water that had been in Fly Car's motor.

Eli swept away the straw under the stairs that concealed the secret compartment, opened the cellar hatch, grabbed the tackle box, and removed the magical silver key to Fly Car. Once more he slid into the driver's seat, slipped the key into the ignition, and cranked it in a clockwise motion.

The car responded with a sputtering sound, like an old-fashioned coffeepot percolating its brew, but that was all. He turned the ignition off, then tried once again.

"Come on, please work," he said, cranking the key. The car sputtered once more, then magically came back to life.

Eli was never so thankful in his entire life. Grady entered the barn just in time to experience Fly Car showing signs of life.

"Well, I'll be." Grady smiled at Eli, admiring his resourcefulness.

That's not to say there wasn't any damage to the vehicle. The right wing looked like an aluminum can that had been ripped in half and needed to be replaced, but that was a minor procedure. Eli collected more cans for the necessary repairs, and Grady reworked the pulley system. After a couple of weeks, the car was almost as good as new.

The completion of the adjustments to the vehicle coincided nicely with Eli's promotion from elementary to middle school. The graduation ceremony was held in the Thomas Edison gym. Three rows of risers were set up. Eli's parents and Grady came a bit early, so they could find seats together.

In front was a podium bedecked with navy streamers and metallic gold stars, and next to it was a display of the graduating kids' pictures and their answers to the question "Where will you be in twenty years?" Eli had said he'd like to be an inventor. A knowing grin spread across Grady's face when he saw the display. "I bet you will be, Junior," he whispered under his breath.

At the reception after the ceremony, Eli went up to Murph to offer him some lemonade and cookies. Murph had other celebration plans: he was taking the helium balloons off the gym wall, inhaling the inert gas, and talking in a comical high-pitched tone. Eli couldn't help but laugh at his best friend's goofy ways.

Eli woke the next day glad to be done with elementary school, as now he could work for most of the day on his dream of a flying car. He had a few new ideas about how to attain the necessary clearance over the wall of black gum trees. They were a menacing obstacle, as formidable as the Great Wall of China.

Eli correctly reckoned that Fly Car needed more propulsion and less weight to clear the grove. Once more he thought about jet packs. Fly Car didn't need much of a boost, he guessed; just thirty seconds or less of additional propulsion would likely lift it a hundred feet higher, so it could soar over the row of trees.

Grady agreed, so the pair began preparing the transformed car for the second test flight. This time they equipped the underbelly of the vehicle with two mini–rocket boosters stocked with thirty seconds' worth of propellant, much like a Harrier aircraft.

Eli was pleased with this first phase of the revisions for the new and improved Fly Car. Phase two would not be so easy to implement, though, so he prepared his case like the best litigator money could buy. "I've been looking at the weight calculations for Fly Car," he said to Grady one day, "and I think the next flight stands the best chance of succeeding if there's only one person in the car—just the pilot," Eli said.

"Is that so?" Grady asked.

"Yep, and since I weigh at least sixty pounds less than you do, give or take a few, I believe I should be the one to test-fly Fly Car."

"That right?"

"So what do you think?"

"I don't like it one bit, but I agree with your analysis, Junior," Grady said reluctantly. "I think if the weather holds, we should give it a go in the morning around 8 a.m."

"Eight o'clock it is."

Eli couldn't sleep that night, thinking about the test flight that lay ahead in the morning. Butterflies tickled his stomach, just as they did on Christmas Eve. The black canvas of night gave way to a pre-dawn indigo as Eli threw on his clothes. It made no sense for him to be up this early, yet there he was, awake with the paper boys, bread deliverers, and mail trucks making their early morning rounds.

To calm his nerves, Eli pretended it was just another day. He went down to the kitchen and poured himself a bowl of cereal. He liked sugary cereal that came in colorful boxes, with cartoon characters on the sides. He completed the maze and word search on the back of the box. After slurping down his last spoonful of sweetened milk, he rinsed out his bowl and placed his spoon on the drying rack.

He opened the front door to check the weather. The sky was clear, with a coral hue that hugged and outlined the trees. A slight wind was blowing from the north, but all in all it felt very manageable.

Eli walked halfway around the circular driveway and grabbed the local newspaper off the cobblestones. He loved reading the cartoons, so he passed the next thirty minutes trying to get his mind off the upcoming event and onto something lighthearted.

The bell on the grandfather clock rang eight chimes, signaling that it was time. Eli got up from the couch, put on his sneakers, and headed out through the mud room to the barn out back.

Grady was waiting for him in the barn. He greeted Eli with a cup of hot chocolate with whipped cream on top. Eli gulped it down, remembering the results of the first ride as he garnered his courage to take the second flight. Working together, Grady and Eli maneuvered Fly Car out the double doors of the barn and onto the lawn in one smooth motion, just as they had done eight weeks earlier.

Eli slipped into the driver's seat, fastened his seat belt, and switched on the ignition. He pressed the wing control button and the doors quickly responded by rocking into position, first forward and then back. Eli touched the button a second time, and the wing tips extended to create a very convincing aircraft. The Plexiglas sliders filled the previous void where the car doors had been just a few moments ago, and Eli was ready for takeoff.

He reluctantly gunned the gas pedal all the way down to the floor. The car accelerated rapidly through the field, with the speedometer increasing ten miles per hour every ten yards. Eli gently pulled back the steering wheel and felt the front tires calmly lifting off the ground.

"Be patient," he thought to himself. When he felt the back tires separate from the lawn, he instinctively pressed the brand-new propulsion button right by the turn signal. Fly

Car responded immediately to the quick burst of thrust and lifted upward about a hundred feet, clearing the black gum grove easily.

The trees swayed as the car flew over them in the early morning air. Eli banked the car ever so slightly to his left, just enough to give a quick wave to Grady, who was looking up from the lawn with a pair of binoculars. He responded with a thumbs-up before quickly setting down the field glasses and picking up a video recorder to capture the moment.

Eli's heart surged with pride as he looped around the suburban neighborhood in Fly Car. He had a picture-perfect bird's-eye view of Thomas Edison Elementary School. He could clearly see Mrs. Fitzgerald's fifth-grade classroom and the neighborhood playground, right next to the grass baseball field where he had saved the game with his snow cone catch.

A few weeks earlier Eli had been a mediocre student in fifth grade, and now he was on the cusp of something big. He noticed Murph's white Craftsman

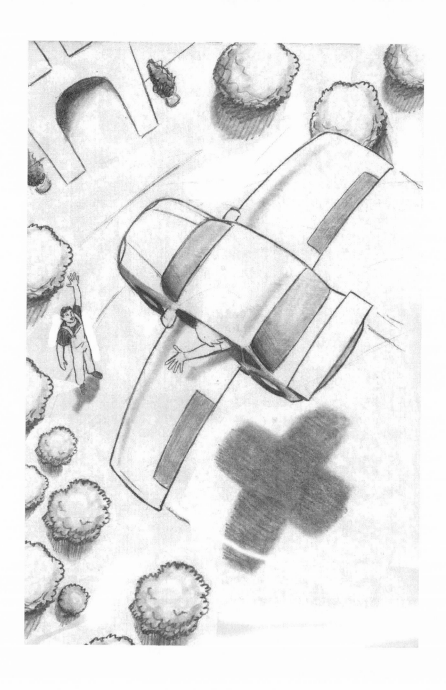

home jutting out from behind a tree-lined street of maples. Eli's world seemed small when he was soaring above it in his latest invention. He had a newfound sense of perspective: "Anything is possible," he thought.

After making a five-minute loop around town, Eli decided to return to Martin Manor. He had read the Greek myth of Daedalus and Icarus, a father and son who try to flee a prison with wings made of wax and feathers. Daedalus warned his son to not fly too close to the sun, lest his waxy wings melt. Unfortunately, the son didn't listen to his father and, tragically, fell into the ocean, never to be heard from again. Eli trusted Grady's words of caution not to push his luck, and was sure he didn't want to tempt fate.

Eli banked Fly Car back toward home and began the descent to the grassy field. He kept the wings as straight as he could while reducing his speed. He placed the flaps in the downward position, which lowered his overall altitude and acceleration.

Eli had played Flight Simulator many times before, but this was the real deal. He was actually landing this car—or was it an aircraft now?

Fly Car continued to soar toward home. The wheels and wings cleared the row of trees. Eli noticed Old Man Murphy's Pond in the three o'clock position. When he was fifty yards to contact, he cut the engine and glided down safely to the ground below. He had accomplished his mission!

Eli turned off the ignition, punched the wing control button twice, and there stood Fly Car safely in the middle of the perfectly manicured lawn. Grady came over to congratulate him on his successful flight, but he couldn't move. He was sitting frozen inside the driver's seat.

"Come on, champ, you did it!"

"I can't move." Eli had his hands clasped to the wheel like a figure in a wax museum.

"You can do this, son." Grady began peeling back each one of Eli's fingers. When he had removed all ten, he proceeded to unbuckle the seat belt and pivot Eli out of the vehicle by rotating his legs.

Just then, Eli's dad sauntered from around the barn and up behind Grady and Eli.

"What exactly are you two doing with my car?"

Eli quickly sprang into action with a speech he'd been rehearsing. "Dad, what's the most precious commodity that you possess?"

"Time, I suppose."

"Exactly." Eli triumphantly extended his index finger and wiggled it. "My goal was to get you some of your life back. Father Time can't reverse the clock, but you can at least maximize the time you still have on this planet."

"Oh, really? And how's that?"

"Great question, Dad. What's the biggest time suck in your day?"

"Definitely my commute."

"Right again. I calculated your average commute time per day. What if I told you there's a way for you to get roughly 167 hours of your life back each year?"

"How?"

"Remember when you took me to the Museum of Flight in Seattle over Labor Day weekend a few years back?" Eli asked.

"Yeah, I do. It was a drizzly day, if I remember correctly."

"Precisely. Remember the Taylor Aerocar III, the prototype that could convert from a car into an airplane in five minutes?"

"Yeah, yeah. That was really an amazing vehicle."

"Well, I hope you don't mind, but instead of five minutes, Grady and I were able to reduce the conversion rate from car to plane down to fifteen *seconds*." Eli shrugged his shoulders. "And by the way, we used the Martin Mercurio to complete the project. We call it Fly Car now."

"You knew about this?" Dad asked.

Grady raised his palms skyward and shrugged his shoulders in a surrender position.

"This is just a *little* bit different than helping Eli with the vinegar and chalk volcano project at last year's science

124

fair," Dad said, putting his index finger and thumb almost together.

Eli's dad did an informal inspection of Fly Car. He walked around the entire vehicle looking for any dents or dings, the way a rental car agent looks over a returned vehicle at the airport. Finally, he ran his hand softly over the hood in a gesture of affection.

Grady resumed his conversation with Eli's dad. "Your boy just wants to spend a little more time with you, Michael. This is his Father's Day gift to you."

"Does it work?" Dad asked.

"Do you want to give it a whirl, or watch the video Grady just took of our second test flight?" Eli asked, grasping his dad's hand.

"Sure. What happened on the first test flight?" Dad asked.

"You don't want to know," Grady and Eli simultaneously replied.

They went inside and settled in the family room. Grady hooked up the video recorder to the oversized plasma television, pressed the rewind button, and then started the footage. Eli's dad sat on the leather sofa, stupefied by what he was watching.

Five minutes later, the video concluded when Eli safely landed Fly Car in the backyard. Grady pressed the stop button and quietly exited the room to give father and son some much-needed time together. Eli's dad jumped up excitedly, as if he'd been shot out of a circus cannon.

"Why didn't I think of this?" he said, his mind racing.

"Invention always seems obvious after the fact," Eli said, reaching up and patting his dad's shoulder.

"Have you told anyone about your little experiment here?" Dad asked.

"No," Eli said matter-of-factly.

"Well, what are you going to do now?" Dad was now pacing back and forth across the family room like a caged lion.

"What I want to do is give you back your car so you can commute to and from work really fast, but ..." Eli left the sentence hanging.

"But what?" Dad asked

"There's still one little hiccup with Fly Car," Eli confessed.

"What's that?" Dad asked, looking even more engaged.

"How to land it on top of the Martin Motors corporate office downtown," Eli said.

"Any ideas?" Dad knew this question always brought out the best in his son.

Eli snapped his fingers at once. "Aircraft carriers."

"What? You lost me there."

"Aircraft carriers use massive hooks to stop a fighter jet's forward motion and keep them from falling off the sides of the flight deck."

"That's true. What would you suggest we do?"

"We need to build a hook mechanism on top of Martin Motors," Eli said. That way you'll be able to safely land Fly Car on the flat surface of the building, and the series of hooks will help halt its forward motion, so it won't fly off the side of the building during your morning commute."

"Hmm," Dad said.

"You'll use the hook system and additional propellant to catapult the car off the side of the building when you head home at the end of the day. How does that sound?" Eli looked at his father expectantly.

"Risky, son, really risky."

Nevertheless, Eli's dad was willing to try to make Fly Car work. He put his best engineers on the project, giving them top security clearances. The team worked tirelessly to come up with a mechanism that would stop the forward progress of Fly Car as the vehicle made its way down for landing in spaces not much larger than a helicopter pad, and then to propel it forward off the roof. Six weeks later, Project Rush Hour was ready to test.

His father decided that the downtown test flight should be on July 4. It would be quieter around the city early in the morning on a holiday, and it would cast the event in a patriotic glow.

Once again Eli was given the lead role as test pilot, since he was the only one who had successfully landed the craft. He agreed on one condition: no media. His dad pushed back, but Eli could be stubborn and convincing when he wanted to, and so they came to an agreement.

Eli was beginning to get a little suspicious of his father's motives for Fly Car. The launch seemed less about patriotism and more about future profits for Martin Motors. His dad had even told Grady and Eli that he was going to get Fly Car patented as an invention under their names.

"Why?" Eli asked. "You're just going to use it to get to and from work, right? What's the big deal?"

"You don't want anyone stealing your idea, do you?" Dad said.

"I guess not."

"Remember the minivan, Grady?" His dad was recalling the incident from Grady's days as a line worker.

"Sure do, sir," Grady declared.

"Great. Then it's settled. We'll get Fly Car patented in the morning." Eli's dad closed the deal by rubbing his son's spiky brown hair.

After Eli's dad left the room, Grady and Eli looked at each other, dumbfounded. Grady put his fingers up to his lips to signal that Eli should not speak until the coast was clear. "Was it me, or did that seem a little weird?" he said in a low voice.

"Definitely different," Eli said.

Even though their names were on Fly Car's patent, they couldn't help but feel that Michael Martin was in the driver's seat when it came to their invention.

Chapter 14

The Eagle Has Landed

Eli woke up early on the morning of Independence Day. Taking Fly Car on a five-minute test loop was one thing, but landing the vehicle successfully on top of a skyscraper smack dab in the middle of downtown Detroit was a completely different challenge.

First off, Eli remembered that landing the plane hadn't been his strongest part of the test flight. Second, if he didn't stick the landing, the consequences could be dire. Still, he felt fairly confident in his ability to successfully complete the mission.

Eli decided to repeat his pre-flight routine. He was a little superstitious, so he put on the exact same clothes he'd worn during his successful solo flight. Then he went downstairs, poured himself a bowl of cereal, read the comics, and prepared himself for the big day ahead. Forty-five minutes later he quietly snuck out back, so his mom wouldn't awaken, and went over to the old barn, as he had done so many times before during the past few months.

Eli found Grady going over the final run-through and cross-checks to make sure that Fly Car was ready for takeoff and landing.

"Is it time?" Eli reluctantly asked.

"Are you sure you want to do this, Eli?" Grady asked.

"Grady, why did you take the job at Martin Motors after your dad died?"

"Because I had to, son. There were mouths to feed and bills to pay." Grady looked quizzically at Eli, wondering why he was asking that question at this moment.

"Yeah, yeah ... I know all that stuff, but beyond that. How did you feel that day you mentioned minivans to my dad?" Eli pushed back.

"Proud that I made a difference," Grady responded.

"That's the exact same reason I need to get behind the wheel and do this," Eli said, looking determined.

Grady and Eli rolled Fly Car out through the double doors of the barn and into the early dawn air. Eli slipped on a pair of shiny black leather racing gloves, fastened his seat belt, and fired up the ignition.

The engine responded with a light roar as he stepped on the gas pedal a couple of times. He didn't need to be reminded that this would be no Sunday drive out in the country.

Grady rubbed Eli's spiky hair. "Good luck, Junior."

"Thanks, Grady. See you later!" Eli said, sounding more confident than he felt.

Eli released the emergency brake and began accelerating down the lawn. He pulled back on the steering wheel ever so slightly, and the front wheels began to leave the ground. One hundred yards more and the back wheels followed suit. Eli was airborne. He pressed the propulsion button and cleared the hedge of trees as if this were his three-thousandth flight in Fly Car instead of his third. Once again, he banked to the left and waved at Grady, who returned the gesture with a snappy salute befitting the Fourth of July.

Ten minutes later, Eli was soaring over the meandering emerald green waterway that was the Detroit River. He noticed seven steel and glass buildings standing like sentries protecting the city, and knew at once that they were part of the famed Renaissance Center. He admired their architecture and could even see the reflection of Fly Car in the windows between the fiftieth and fifty-first floor of the center's hotel, the Detroit Marriott.

Eli negotiated his way around the historic sites of the city. He flew by One Detroit Center and the Penobscot Building before making a ninety-degree turn to pass the Book Tower and City Center.

He spotted Martin Motors' corporate headquarters in the middle of downtown with relative ease. It was a modest building in comparison to some of Detroit's skyscrapers, but it had a feature that many of the other buildings lacked: a flat, open roof that was perfect for a landing strip, now modified just for Fly Car.

Eli leaned heavily on his instrumentation to get him though the landing. Keeping the wings as steady as he could, he grasped the steering wheel as if his life depended upon it—which it actually did.

He made the descent slowly but surely. At about a hundred yards from the edge of the building, he eased the steering wheel down cautiously. Seconds later, Fly Car's tires screeched and smoked as they kissed the blacktop. The hook device engaged, snatched the vehicle, and brought the car to an immediate halt.

The action all happened rapidly and rather violently. Eli's head smacked against the front windshield with a loud crack. It wasn't enough to splinter the glass, but it caused an egg-shaped lump to form on his forehead.

A throng of media photographers immediately emerged from behind a covered rooftop staircase, startling Eli. Hadn't his dad promised there'd be no media?

Reporters bombarded Eli with questions as he exited Fly Car. He did his best to cover the corner of his forehead with an extended arm as he waved to the crowd. Cameras flashed as if it were Oscar night and Eli a celebrity strolling down the red carpet.

Eli tried to act enthusiastic for the media, but behind the jovial exterior he was furious at his father. Later, behind closed doors, he let his dad have the full measure of his fury.

"I thought we had a deal. No media!"

"I know, I know, but Martin Motors' stock price is in the tank. Shareholders are unhappy, and if you haven't heard, we're near bankruptcy. Don't you think we should give everyone something to smile about?"

Eli didn't like his father's reasoning. All he'd wanted was a little more time with his dad, and now what he'd hoped would be a father-and-son bonding opportunity was turning into a media circus. If he'd known his father had staged this event to boost the stock price and appease shareholders, he wouldn't have made the daring journey at all.

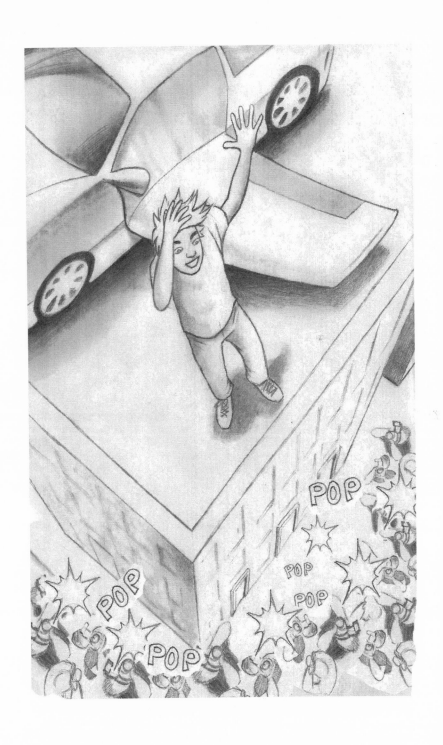

After the photographers and reporters dispersed, Eli and his dad returned to Martin Manor in stony silence. Their sedan pulled into the circular driveway, past the decorative fountain, toward the front door. Eli's dad stooped at the doorstep to pick up the *Wall Street Journal*.

The two were met at the door by Eli's mom, who wasn't too pleased to see the growing purple bruise on her only child's forehead.

"What happened to Eli?"

"He had a little accident," Dad replied, looking down nervously while wiping his feet on an oversized area rug in the hallway.

"I can see that. Does he have a concussion?" his mom said in a concerned tone as she inspected Eli's forehead, which was now aching.

"I'm not sure. I'm not a doctor," Dad said.

"Before *you* go around using *our* son as a test pilot, I'd appreciate it if *we* could at least have a conversation about it," Mom said, fixing her eyes on her husband.

"How did you know?"

"Seriously, Michael? I just turned on the television. The Fly Car story is on every channel across America," Mom replied as she stormed into the living room to fetch her purse. "I'm taking Eli to the doctor to get checked out."

Chapter 15

The Show Must Go On

Eli and his dad were inundated with requests for interviews and appearances after footage of Fly Car's flight went viral on the Internet. They spent the rest of the summer on a media tour—the *Today* show, *Good Morning America*, the afternoon talk shows, local television stations, talk radio.

New York, Boston, and Philadelphia were part of their East Coast excursion. A Southern swing followed, with visits to Atlanta, Orlando, and Miami. Next they hit the Midwest: Minneapolis, Chicago, and Dallas. And then they went out west to Phoenix, Las Vegas, and the late-night shows in Los Angeles.

Eli was happy to be spending more time with his dad, but he felt a bit like a circus performer—wheeled out for his act, and then motored back to the confines of a hotel room, where he would order meals from room service. Hopping from hotel to hotel across the country made him long for his own life back home.

It wouldn't have been so bad if he didn't have to answer the same questions over and over: "What inspired you to create Fly Car?" "When did you know it was going to work?" "Tell us about your co-inventor, Grady."

At times, Eli wished he were just back in the barn with Grady fine-tuning Fly Car. "Life was a whole lot simpler six months ago," he thought. He was beginning to understand why celebrities crave anonymity. It seemed like there was always another question to answer, another program to shoot, another photograph to take, another autograph to sign.

Finally, though, it was time to head home. Eli had spent eight weeks stumping for Fly Car with his dad. Both Martins were exhausted from the demanding schedule, but the cross-country media blitz had helped stabilize Martin Motors' stock price. As the two took their seats for their flight from Los Angeles to Detroit, Eli's dad leaned over and spoke to him.

"Hey, I wanted to thank you for helping out the company."

Eli glared. "That's great, Dad, but what about me?"

Dad looked puzzled. "What about you? Don't you know that you're famous now?"

Eli looked out of the airplane window and then turned back to his dad. "Who cares? I'd gladly trade it all in for thirty minutes out in the barn with Grady."

"Well, in a couple of hours you'll get your wish." With that, his dad opened his laptop and went back to work.

Eli was eager to blend back into the woodwork and be just another kid from suburban Detroit getting ready for the start of middle school. Soon after he and his dad arrived home, he headed over to Murph's house for some normalcy. What he liked most about hanging with his friend was that it was never complicated. Murph didn't ask a million questions, even after all the hullabaloo.

The two boys decided to head back to Martin Manor and fish at Old Man Murphy's Pond. The young fishermen cast their lines into the tea-brown water. The pond was not quite opaque and had a translucent layer that twinkled in the sun. The lead weights made a simultaneous gentle plunk in the water. The boys pulled up a seat under the shady protection of the mature willow tree. This time it was Eli's turn to play interviewer. "So what have you been up to this summer?"

"Not much. Our Little League all-star team made it to the state championship game, but lost in the finals to Grand Rapids. The opposing manager told his pitchers to walk me every time, so I didn't even get to bat," Murph said disappointedly.

"Anything else?"

"Abigail Anderson threw a party for her twelfth birthday," Murph said excitedly.

"Isn't that just another way of saying she had a birthday party?" Eli said, with a bit of superiority in his tone.

"Who are you, my mother?" Murph responded.

"Sorry! Go on."

"Well, Madison asked Abigail what she wanted most for her birthday, and she said she wished Eli Martin would ask her out. What do you think of that?"

"No way."

"Way."

Just then, Eli felt a strong pull coming from the murky waters. He reeled in his pole and saw a nice-sized bass on the other end of the line. As the fish jumped out of the water and fell back into the pond, Eli realized this might be the catch of the day. There was quite a bit of fight in this fella.

As the creature was wiggling closer to shore, Murph grabbed the metallic silver net and scooped up the fish in one fell swoop, as if he was catching a routine pop fly. Eli unclasped the hook from the right side of the squiggly aquatic critter's cheek and released the fish back into Old Man Murphy's Pond.

"Hey, what did you do that for?" Murph questioned.

After all that Eli had been through this busy summer, he answered Murph's question the only way he knew how: honestly.

"I guess I just wanted him to feel free," he said philosophically.

Chapter 16

Rite of Passage

Summer came and went, and now middle school was on the near horizon. Eli and Murph continued their morning routine of heading off together for the first day of school at Henry Ford Middle School, just as they had done during their elementary years at Edison.

Eli was thankful to have a hulking friend as a middle school bodyguard. Part of the education of middle school would be learning how to negotiate the "danger zones," which Murph described as the crossroads where the wrong place meets up with the wrong time.

Eli and Murph were pretty quick studies of the middle school landscape, so they quickly learned that the best way to survive sixth grade was to stick together or travel in a pack. Every once in a while, though, isolation couldn't be helped.

One day Eli was called out of homeroom to go to the orthodontist. He was having a first appointment for braces.

Stopping in the boys' bathroom first, he was accosted by an eighth-grader who seemed to be loitering there, playing hooky from class.

"Well, well, well … what do we have here?," said the eighth-grader. "If it isn't the inventor geek of the year. I saw you on television this summer. Bet you wish you had Fly Car right now to whoosh you out of here." He knocked Eli's textbooks out of his arms.

Out of thin air, the assistant principal arrived on the scene and began questioning the pair. "Where are you supposed to be, son?" he asked Eli.

"I'm trying to get to my orthodontist appointment."

"Well, you better get going, young man, or you're going to be late."

Gratefully, Eli picked up his school supplies and scooted down the hallway and out the double doors. As he glanced back, he was pleased to see the eighth-grader being escorted to the office for further questioning.

Eli briskly jogged to his family's black sedan with its personalized MRTNMOM license plate, hopped into the passenger seat, and slammed the door.

"You look a little harried. Is everything okay?" Mom asked.

"Fine," Eli lied.

"How are you feeling about getting braces?"

"Necessary evil, I guess."

"Let me get a quick look at that smile, because I won't be seeing it for much longer," Mom teased.

All was quiet for a few minutes as they made their way to the orthodontist's office. Eli was glad for the chance to gather his thoughts.

When he wasn't brainstorming new ways to survive sixth grade, Eli was wondering what had happened to Fly Car. He knew his dad had begun taking it to and from work every day, and it had attracted attention. People were talking about it as the next wave of transportation. Some thought the car and airplane makers could merge, creating a hybrid vehicle that would reduce traffic and help families have more time together.

Eli was torn on this concept. He had built Fly Car to give his father more time to spend with him, but instead his dad was spending his increased free time on his smart phone and work. All Eli's invention had done, it seemed, was make his father even busier as an executive and less available as a dad.

"Could we go to a Tigers game?" Eli asked.

"I thought you didn't like baseball," Mom said.

"I don't, but Dad does … so I thought we could all go as a family. You know talk, eat peanuts and popcorn, maybe catch a foul ball."

"Okay, okay. I'll run it by your father." Mom smiled as she dropped Eli off for his appointment.

That Friday night, the Tigers were opening a series against the New York Yankees. Eli and his mom were all set to meet his dad at the ballpark, since the stadium was only ten blocks away from Martin Motors' corporate headquarters.

But his dad had reserved a luxury box for the ballgame and invited some of his fellow executives and board members to attend. "This is going to be just like work," Eli thought, "with my dad running around and holding court with a bunch of businessmen in suits. The game will just be white noise in the background."

Sure enough, Eli was right. He had become pretty skilled at eavesdropping on adult conversations. Although he didn't completely understand the exchanges between the men, who spoke in business jargon and low whispers, he did get the gist of what they were saying. Key words like "scalable," "production schedules," and "FAA approval" danced in his ears. But it was a comment by his father to a neighboring business titan that really ticked off Eli. Apparently his dad was betting the entire company's future on a new and improved Fly Car for the upcoming model year.

Eli didn't know what to think. He felt honored to be part of a long line of Martin men who had kept the family company alive for the next generation. But he also felt his creativity was being exploited by his father to make money for the company. His stomach twitched. He asked his mom if they could head home.

"But we haven't even made it to the seventh-inning stretch. Don't you want to sing 'Take Me Out to the Ballgame'?" Mom asked.

"Nah, I just want to go."

His mom quickly went over to his dad and lightly tapped him on his shoulder. He nodded and excused himself from the circle of executives, who were speaking excitedly in low voices.

"Michael, I'm going to take Eli home. He's pretty wiped out from the week and going to the ortho," she said.

"Sure, sure. I understand." He gave her a quick hug.

Eli and his mom exited the ballpark while his dad and the executives talked throughout the entire evening. They completely missed an exciting come-from-behind victory by the Tigers. When the game ended, they gave a polite golfer's clap and moved toward their luxury vehicles in the nearby reserved parking lot.

Eli asked a lot of questions on the ride home. "Mom, did you know that Dad was planning on bringing Fly Car into full-scale production?"

"Your father is pretty tight-lipped when it comes to running the family business, Eli," Mom offered.

"Yeah, I know all that, but what did your sixth sense tell you? You've always had good intuition when it comes to reading Dad."

"I suspected he'd try to save the company by bringing Fly Car to market." Mom sighed dejectedly. She was torn between her love for Eli and defending her husband's mission to save Martin Motors.

"Without my permission," Eli said testily.

"Yep." Mom sounded conflicted. Eli knew she was bracing for the storm to come.

"When did you know?"

"I had a feeling that was his plan when he started pushing you to get Fly Car patented," Mom said.

"Why didn't you tell me?"

"I was hoping that maybe, just maybe, history might be different this time."

Eli looked skeptical.

"Now, before you flip your switch, Eli, I want you to consider this," Mom said. "Your father is trying to save the jobs of twenty thousand employees. You like Grady, right? Well, your dad is not just doing this entirely for the money. He has to look into the eyes of thousands of Gradys every day when he walks the assembly line. Does that make any sense?"

"Yeah, I get it. I guess somebody has to be the CEO's son, but it doesn't mean I have to like it." Eli looked down at the ground. He'd have given anything right then to have a regular family, not a family whose whole world revolved around Martin Motors. "One more question, Mom, and that's it."

"Sure, Eli."

"I thought I overheard Dad discussing the patent with one of the board members. I could have sworn I heard him say that the name Michael Martin was on the official document. Do you know anything about this?"

"What your dad does at work is his business," Mom replied.

"Mom, we were supposed to be going to a Tigers game as a family tonight. A luxury suite is not supposed to be the Martin Motors boardroom, and besides, *I* invented Fly Car." Eli pounded the armrest for emphasis.

Just then the black sedan pulled into the circular driveway of Martin Manor. Eli ran up to his room. It didn't take him too long to figure out exactly what he needed to do next.

He waited until the house was completely quiet. Then he snuck out the back screen door and down into the barn. He pointed his security-sized metallic red flashlight at the wooden rooster and plucked the keys to the double barn doors from underneath it. He slid the doors open carefully and found Fly Car comfortably tucked into the barn for the night.

Eli swiftly swept away the hay under the stairs that led to the loft. He lifted the trap door, grabbed for the tackle box, and flipped the brass levers on its sides simultaneously. Sitting right in its usual spot was the key to the flying machine. Swooping down in a single motion, Eli snatched it up.

Next he flipped the car cover to the ground and gave Fly Car a long, admiring look before sliding into the familiar rich black leather driver's seat. With a deep breath, he slipped the key into the ignition and moved the shifter into the neutral position. After depressing the emergency brake, he pushed with all his might and was able to get the car out of the barn without making too much noise.

Once he was clear of the barn, he calmly thought through his plan. He would accelerate the car down the lawn at full speed, place an old ten-pound cast iron weight he'd found in the barn onto the gas pedal, and hop out at the last minute, causing Fly Car to bound into Old Man Murphy's Pond and find its final resting place at the bottom of the murky depths.

Eli started the car with a loud revving of the engine. It felt rebellious and right to be making such a loud racket at this late hour of the night. Peering in the rearview mirror, he noticed that a light had immediately turned on in the master bedroom of Martin Manor. With a newfound sense of urgency, he slammed the automatic shifter into drive and pushed the gas pedal down to the floor. Fly Car rapidly responded and began roaring down the lawn at top speed.

Eli had rolled down the driver's-side window of the car, and the night air felt chilly on his bare arms as it rushed by. Goose bumps were forming on his skin, but he wasn't sure if they were due to the temperature or the upcoming trouble he soon would be facing. He prepared himself for the impact upon a sudden exit.

Eli had once seen a stunt show at an amusement park that had captivated him. He had learned how movie and TV stunt people fell in a certain way to prevent injuries when filming a dangerous scene. Now he was planning to imitate what he'd seen—in particular, the hit-and-roll technique he'd seen at the show.

Eli shoved the cast iron weight onto the gas pedal and took his foot off the gas. At the last possible second, he leaned into the door and made his high-speed escape. The soft grass buffered some of the blow, but the landing still knocked the wind out of him. He rolled six consecutive times and stopped just in time to see Fly Car float off the edge of the bank, soar through the night air, and slam headfirst into Old Man Murphy's Pond.

Chapter 17

Grounded for Life

Eli smiled with satisfaction as he saw Fly Car begin to submerge in the murky water. The open windows made the car sink quickly. He watched the taillights fade to black as they descended into the depths of the pond. Just then, his dad came storming out of the house in his robe and slippers, disheveled and angry.

"What the heck do you think you're doing?" Dad yelled.

"How come we never go fishing anymore?" Eli screamed back, matching his father's volume.

"What does that have to do with this?" Dad sputtered in confusion, pointing to the gurgling bubbles caused by the submerged car.

"You heard me. We used to go fishing all the time in this exact place. Now all you care about is seeing your face on the cover of *Business Weekly* or *Fortune* magazine."

"It's not that like that, Eli. Your great-grandfather started something right back there." He pointed to the barn. "Now he has left that legacy for me to continue. Do you have any clue how difficult that is?" Dad ran his hand through his disheveled hair.

"Do you have any idea what it's like to have a dad who's never around or when he is around, he's completely checked out?" Eli yelled back. "I made Fly Car so you could spend more time with us, but all you did was fill the time with more work! Forget it—I'm outta here."

Eli started marching angrily toward Martin Manor. All of a sudden his dad took off running after him. He grabbed the boy by his arm to turn him around.

"Do you have any idea what it's like to keep a teetering company off life support?" Dad said. "I'm doing this for you—can't you understand that?"

"No, you're not," Eli said. "Do you remember a couple of years ago, when I was eight years old and in the Cub Scouts?"

"Yes," Dad responded cautiously, uncertain where his son was heading.

"I'm sure you can recall the Pinewood Derby race."

"Yes, what about it?"

"What did you do, Dad?" Eli responded.

"I dunno. I'm guessing we raced the model cars down the hilled track." Dad scratched his head.

"Dad, let me explain this event from my perspective, and I just want you to try to listen, okay?"

"Okay."

"Murph and I were both pretty excited to receive our Pinewood Derby race-car kits at our Cub Scout pack meeting. Murph's dad was out of town on an International flight, so Murph just made his car the best he could, remember?"

"Oh yeah, Murph's car was a real piece of junk, if I remember correctly." Dad chuckled at the memory.

"Then what did you do, Dad?" Eli quickened his pace of questioning.

"Your guess is as good as mine." Dad sounded embarrassed.

"Well, I'll tell you. The next day my Pinewood Derby kit mysteriously disappeared. I thought maybe, just maybe, I left it over at Murph's house, but Mom noticed that you had placed the materials in your briefcase as you headed off to work the next morning. What did you do?"

"I'm listening."

"You had a group of your best engineers create the most aerodynamic Pinewood Derby race car ever. You even had them run it through a wind tunnel, place graphite on the wheels to reduce friction, and paint it perfectly." Eli's memory was as painstakingly accurate as his father's was nonexistent.

"So what's wrong with that?" Dad was growing impatient.

"Dad, building a Pinewood Derby car is something most fathers and sons do *together*. It's supposed to be one of those father-and-son experiences like building a campfire."

"Hmm," Dad said. There was a long pause. "Point well taken."

"Do you remember what happened on racing day?" Eli asked.

"We were creamed by Murph and his block of wood with wheels," Dad said, shaking his head.

"Exactly. The point is, Dad, you took my car and tried to win at all costs. Don't do that again." With that final comment, Eli sprinted into the darkness toward Martin Manor.

"Wait! I can explain everything," Dad blurted into the night air, but it was too late. This time it was Eli's turn to disappear.

Chapter 18

That's What Friends Are For

Eli sprinted into the warm summer night with a sense of purpose. He was running as fast as his ten-year-old legs could carry him.

His mind raced back to the memory of the timed mile that the school ran once a year in PE. Eli always liked the feeling of pushing himself when running longer distances. He remembered always being toward the back of his class after the first lap.

Fortunately, the mile required four trips around the Edison Elementary cinder track. By the second lap, Eli would move up toward the middle of the pack of joggers. By the third lap, the kids who didn't pace themselves properly would start fading to the back. Murph was one of those kids, huffing and puffing as he watched his best friend breeze past his right shoulder.

Eli was just the opposite. His boundless energy and light weight were an asset as he made his way toward the front of the fifth-graders. He'd complete lap four in a full sprint. Last year, the timed mile had come down to Eli and Connor Larson, a skinny eleven-year-old whose dad was the cross-country coach at a neighboring high school. Eli remembered the race being a back-and-forth battle between the two runners, with Connor nosing him out at the finish line, but not before they had both beat the previous Edison school record for fastest timed mile.

He was still irritated at having been beaten, though. He redoubled his sprint toward the one person he could count on to welcome him at this time of night: his buddy Murph.

Eli ran around the back of the Murphys' house and tapped on the window of Murph's bedroom, which was in a daylight basement. Murph groggily got out of bed and slid open the window.

"What are you doing?" he said, rubbing his eyes and yawning open-mouthed, as if awakening from hibernation.

"Just needed some space. Can I spend the night here?" Eli asked.

"Dude, you smell. Go take a shower. Here are some PJs." Murph thrust a pair of plaid pajamas in Eli's direction.

As Eli was cleaning up, there was a light tap on the Murphys' door. Michael Martin was waiting on the doorstep, exhausted, when Gene Murphy opened the front door. Michael looked like an exhausted father desperate to find his only child. Gene gave a tired yawn, just as his son had a few moments before.

"Well, hello, Michael. What brings you by?" Gene said. "It's not every night that a Fortune 500 CEO drops by a neighbor's house close to midnight to borrow some sugar."

"Is Eli here?"

"Not that I know of. What's up?"

"He crashed the car into Old Man Murphy's Pond, then ran off," Michael said. "I don't know where he went—and it's almost midnight!"

"I bet he's fine. Your son is a resourceful boy. But I'll help you look for him." Gene gathered his robe and slippers, and the two men began to scour the neighborhood.

As the cold night air woke him up and he gathered his senses, Gene thought he could guess where Eli had gone. He texted his wife, and she texted back in a minute with a confirmation.

"Michael, great news!," Gene said. "Eli is over at our house after all."

"Thank God!" Michael said. "Thanks, man. I was so worried."

"Michael, I don't mean to jump into your family business, but I want to ask you a question, if I could."

"Sure."

"Do you know why my son Earl is such a good baseball player?"

"What does this have to do with my boy running away?"

"Humor me, Michael."

"Because he's the biggest kid in the league."

"Well, that's part of the answer, but only part," Gene said. "You see, baseball is a game that's passed down from father to son. My old man was a mechanic. Worked with his hands for a living and made an honest man's wage. Spent quite a bit of time under the hood tuning up the cars your dad used to make. No matter how tired he was after his shift, he'd always make time to play catch with me in the backyard.

"Now I try to do the same with Murph when I'm in town. But the reality is I'm not always in town. I'm not saying that baseball has to be your thing with your kid, but what I am saying is we have to do better by our sons. Our boys are almost teenagers, and pretty soon that window will be closed forever, as their friends take over our place in their lives. Something to think about."

"I would like to, I really would, but our company is on the verge of complete financial collapse," Michael confessed.

"That's tough stuff, Michael, it really is. But life is full of decisions. What you give time to is what you ultimately value. While we're having this truth-telling moment, I'll share mine. The problem is, I can't be in two places at once. Trust me, I live with this guilt all the time when I'm on the road, holed up in some hotel in Asia after a fourteen-hour flight across the Pacific Ocean. It's a challenge managing the Tigers from a different continent. No matter how hard I try, the reality is I'm halfway around the globe."

Gene shook his head and then continued. "I like your boy, Michael. He's a really good kid, but he needs his dad just like Earl needs me in his life. It's time for us to move out of the dugout and into the batter's box of parenting before it's too late." He smiled, rather pleased with his analogy.

Michael nodded knowingly. Together they shuffled back to the Murphys' house. The front-door light was collecting moths and the door creaked open as Michael entered the house. He collected his sleeping son in his arms and headed back home.

Chapter 19

Good Advice

The next morning, Eli came downstairs to a breakfast table set with three of his favorite things: his mom, his dad, and a stack of buttermilk pancakes. He stabbed his fork into three of the golden brown discs and placed them on the middle of his plate. He slathered them with butter, salivating as it melted and oozed down the hot stack like molten lava.

Eli piled a swirl of whipped cream on top and added some fresh-cut strawberries for good measure. He began downing his breakfast as if it were an ordinary morning, and he hadn't spent the previous night essentially committing grand theft auto.

Eli's dad ran his fingers through his hair and scratched the whiskers on his chin as he regarded his son. He was still tired, but finally he cleared his throat and began.

"You gave us a pretty good scare last night, Eli."

"And?" Eli responded with the fewest words possible.

"I guess I wanted to know why you'd sabotage your own invention, something you created almost from scratch."

"Dad, I already told you this last night," Eli said. "I created Fly Car for you. So maybe, just maybe, we could get a little more quality time together. But you turned it into the savior of your company. Now I know once and for all where your priorities lie. Can I please be excused?" Eli slammed his plate into the sink and ran out the back door toward the barn.

The doors were still open from the previous night's activity. Grady was sitting on a stool inside.

"Mmm, mmm, mmm … I've done some stupid things in my life, but Junior, what you did last night takes the cake," Grady said.

"I know."

"Your father isn't a perfect man by any stretch of the imagination, but he's a good man. Do you have any idea what he's trying to do?"

Eli shrugged his shoulders.

"He's trying to help save this city. If it weren't for your dad and a few others, Detroit could become a ghost town. Ever heard of Virginia City, Nevada?"

"No," Eli mumbled as he kicked at some straw. He wasn't in the mood for another of Grady's stories.

"At the turn of the twentieth century, when the silver mines in Nevada were at full production, forty thousand people lived up on a hillside town known as Virginia City. Do you know how many people live there today?"

"No."

"Guess?" Grady challenged.

"Two thousand," Eli responded.

"Sorry, son, but thanks for playing along. More like nine hundred. Silver mines dried up and Virginia City became a ghost town. Do you want Detroit to become the next Virginia City?"

"I guess not, but it's not fair. I never get to see my dad. Murph plays catch in the backyard with his father. Do you know who I play catch with? A backstop."

"No one ever said life was fair, son. I started working two days after I graduated from high school and never looked back. Sometimes the world's needs are bigger than your own."

Eli was silent for a moment. "Grady, do you think you could borrow your uncle's tow truck again?"

"Now that's the spirit." Grady broke into a grin.

Chapter 20

Mending Fences

Back at Martin Manor, Eli's mom and dad were having a heart-to-heart talk while clearing the breakfast dishes.

"Michael, I'm sure you know you're jeopardizing your relationship with Eli over this flying car," his mom said.

"I know, I know. I just need to make Eli understand how important this invention is for the Motor City."

"Important for the Motor City or for Martin Motors?"

"Okay, okay, I give up. If I'm drinking truth serum, probably a little bit of both." His dad raised both hands in surrender.

Just then Eli came into the house to grab an apple.

"Can I have a word with you, son?" Dad asked, looking straight into Eli's eyes.

"Sure."

"When I was a kid, my favorite book was *The Phantom Tollbooth* by Norton Juster," Dad said. "In one of the sections, the author wrote about the difference between illusion and reality. There once was this beautiful city with fine houses and inviting spaces, but the residents of the city were in such a hurry to get from destination to destination that they didn't appreciate the beauty the town had to offer. They forgot to take time to look at all of its avenues and wonders.

"And because nobody made time to admire the city, slowly but surely it began to disappear. What was once reality had become an illusion. So what do you think, Eli?"

"It is kind of a cool concept, Dad, but I'm not sure what you're trying to say." Eli took a big bite out of his apple and wiped his mouth with his shirtsleeve.

"Detroit is kind of like that city, Eli. People used to move to Detroit in droves to work for the Big Three automakers. Now our town is fighting for its survival. Whole city blocks are being boarded up, businesses are closing, and you saw firsthand what happened to the old Packard plant. I'm fighting for the Motor City I loved and knew as a kid, so it won't become a mirage."

"Yeah, Dad, that's great and all, but what about me?" Eli responded. He still had chunks of apple in his mouth.

"If you don't mind, Eli, I'd like to tell you one more story."

"Be my guest."

"One Saturday morning, right around the time I finished *The Phantom Tollbooth*, my dad, your grandpa, was sitting on his tractor finishing up mowing the lawn—the very same lawn you used for takeoffs and landings of Fly Car. Anyway, my dad finished up mowing the entire five-acre plot, came in, rubbed my head and told me he loved me, and walked upstairs to his bedroom. That was the one and only time I can remember him clearly saying those words directly to me."

"Those are nice stories, Dad, but I'd like it better if you could try a little harder on the family front, instead of just talking about how hard you're trying. It seems to me the city in *The Phantom Tollbooth* is a lot like our family, actually. But you're only seeing that it's like Detroit." Eli walked out of the room, leaving his dad shaking his head.

Chapter 21

Worlds Collide

On Friday morning, Eli's dad decided to take a chance and ask his son to come to work with him. He knew it was a risky proposition, but he went ahead with the request. Surprisingly, Eli accepted.

Initially, Eli rationalized his decision as a great way to get out of school, but he soon realized it was more than that. His dad had talked about his job, but this was different. Eli would actually be able to see his father in action. He accepted the invitation under one condition: he'd be allowed to shadow his dad for the entire day.

At the appointed hour, the Martin men hopped into the black luxury sedan, wearing matching blue dress shirts and navy slacks, and made their way to the Martin Motors corporate headquarters downtown. As soon as Eli's dad arrived at his office, he was bombarded with questions by staff from the different divisions of his company. Bob from Marketing wanted him to look at the splashy new advertising campaign for the upcoming quarter. Elaine in Accounting wanted to know how they were going to pay for the splashy new ad campaign. Hal from Legal wanted to know what the company's legal obligation would be if it started mass-producing Fly Cars and had an accident using the new technology. Eli's dad did his best to answer each question, most of which required careful consideration and analysis. Finally, he silenced the throng to check in with his son.

"What do you think of all this, Eli?" Dad said.

"How do you do this all day, Dad?" Eli said. "It would drive me nuts."

"Welcome to my world," Dad said. "You get used to it."

By the middle of the day the pace had slowed a bit, and Eli's dad was able to carve out time in his busy schedule to take his son to the cafeteria for lunch. At the end of the meal, Eli slurped the last of his chocolate milk through his straw and began asking some of the questions he'd long had about Dad and his job.

"So Dad, do you like what you do?"

"Most of the time." Dad gave a weary smile.

"Why?" Eli asked.

"Running a company is kind of like solving a thousand-piece puzzle. You have all these departments, which are kind of like pieces, and you have to make all them all fit together to see the whole picture. That's where I come in. I like solving problems," Dad said proudly.

Just as his dad completed his sentence, Eli felt a strange sensation wash over him. For years he'd fought the notion that he was just like his old man, but seeing his dad in action made him realize that maybe, just maybe, they were more alike than he'd ever imagined.

"I'm really glad I came today," Eli said. "I really get what you do now."

"I'm glad you came too," Dad said, grinning. "One day you may be running this baby."

"You gotta be crazy."

"Well, it is the family business," Dad reminded Eli. "And there was one other minor detail I didn't have a chance to fully explain."

"Yeah, what's that?"

"Mom said you overheard me speaking to one of the board members at the ballgame about whose name was on the patent," Dad said.

"That's right, and I heard you say 'Michael Martin,'" Eli said.

"You're right, Eli, but that's not the full story. Michael Martin's name *is* on the patent—Michael Elias Martin." Eli's dad looked over at his son to see his reaction.

"My name?" Eli smiled broadly.

Eli's dad reached over and touched his shoulder. "I knew you'd figure it out, son. That's why Grady is always calling you Junior."

"But what about Grady?"

"Don't worry about Grady. I have big plans for him as well."

That evening Eli fell asleep on the drive home, wiped out after a long day at the office. His dad pulled into the circular driveway in the luxury sedan, turned off the car lights, and gently nudged Eli awake. The two headed into the house together. Eli kicked off his sneakers at the front doorstep, ambled upstairs, pulled the comforter over his shoulders, and immediately went to sleep.

Chapter 22

Back in Business

On Saturday morning, Eli and Grady met at Old Man Murphy's Pond. They were still working on rescuing Fly Car from its murky depths. Having previously pulled the car out of the pond during the middle of the night, Eli had assumed that doing the same thing during the middle of the day would be a piece of cake.

But that hadn't proven to be the case. The car's right front tire had become wedged between a log and a boulder, and it became even more tightly wedged every time they tried to pull it out.

Eli remembered a famous quote by the Greek physicist and engineer Archimedes: "Give me a lever big enough, and I will move the world." Remembering the black iron pole Murph had used as his depth-finding invention a few months back, he ran back to the old barn to fetch it. It was propped in the corner of the barn, right next to an old pitchfork.

Eli walked back down to the pond, placed his scuba mask over his face, and submerged himself next to the cattails and lily pads. Jamming the pole under the boulder, he was able to flip the heavy stone by a quarter turn, thus freeing the vehicle's front tire.

Grady hit the winch, and slowly Fly Car was brought to the surface once again. But Eli didn't feel the sense of excitement or accomplishment that he had the first time they'd raised the red roadster. He still didn't fully trust his dad's intentions.

Grady determined that the car would have to be detailed, dried, and then evaluated for damages. The front axle had received considerable damage, and would need to be straightened and repaired. He took great interest in making sure Fly Car was returned to its previous state. He knew his job depended upon a complete restoration, and besides, it was his invention as well.

In the meantime, Eli's dad made a concerted effort to reach out to his son. Gene's man-to-man pep talk had resonated with him.

One Sunday after church, he took Eli downtown to the research and development wing of Martin Motors. It was a massive white industrial-size hangar within the city confines, surrounded by a twelve-foot electric chain link fence and accessible only with a security clearance.

Eli's dad eased the black sedan up to the front gate, showed the security officer his badge, and was waved through. He pulled up to Building 84 and stopped.

"I renamed our latest research and development office Building 84 because that was the year my dad gave me the Martin Mercurio," Dad said. "Inside, our staff has been analyzing the work you completed on Fly Car and updating the technology. Behind these doors is the future of automotive engineering as we know it." Dad beamed with pride.

Once inside the enormous structure, Eli could see two dozen prototypes of Fly Car in a rainbow of colors. His dad escorted him to a small viewing room, where they watched a five-minute promotional video on the capabilities of the car and the benefits of traveling in it.

Eli attempted to sound enthusiastic. "This is really great, Dad."

"Do you know what this could mean for the city of Detroit?" Dad said. "We're talking a second renaissance here—people coming back to this town—instead of the massive exodus of the past decade. Of course, we need to receive FAA approval." Dad's enthusiasm was filling the whole room.

Eli was beginning to share his dad's excitement. "Okay, but if the FAA approves Fly Car, and Martin Motors can begin full-scale production, you need to promise me something."

"Name it," Dad said.

"You need to purchase and completely renovate the old downtown Packard plant, and make it the home of a state-of-the-art assembly line for Fly Car."

"You know, I always liked that building. We'd need a ton of money to retrofit it, but it could be done," Dad said. "We'd have to run a few quarters in the black, you know, be profitable, before making that kind of investment."

"I know, I know. I've played a few games of Monopoly in my lifetime," Eli said, cracking a smile.

"Deal," Dad said. The two shook hands and headed for the door.

As they made their way back home, they detoured by the old Packard plant and took in its dilapidated state. As if reading his dad's mind, Eli beat him to the punch.

"It doesn't look like much now, but this building can be great again. It just needs to be given a chance."

"Just like Martin Motors?"

"No, actually, more like you, Dad," Eli joked. It was the first time the two had shared a laugh in quite a while.

The sedan made its way around the circular driveway and parked. Eli got out of the car and began running out back toward the barn. He stopped after twenty feet and looked back at his dad.

"Hey, thanks for the field trip," Eli said, then waved and continued toward the barn. His dad quietly whispered under his breath, "No, thank *you*."

"Grady, how's it going with Fly Car?" Eli said. The two of them had been through a lot together, and he wanted to make sure the good times would continue.

"Not too bad," Grady said. "The axle was badly bent, but I took it to a local auto shop and they were able to fix it."

"Dad and I had a good day together," Eli said. "I'm starting to feel better about him mass-producing Fly Car. It seems like it could save Martin Motors and help the city of Detroit too."

"I'm proud of you, son." Grady gave him a fist bump.

"So I guess we go back to the lab again."

"Now you're talking some sense, Junior."

Chapter 23

Things Are Looking Up, Way Up

Grady and Eli spent the better part of a month getting Fly Car back to operational status. Once the axle was straightened, there were some minor adjustments that needed to be made to the propulsion unit underneath the car. The two inventors of Fly Car needed to make sure their creation was still airworthy, because Eli's dad was going to introduce Fly Car as part of a huge media blitz at the Detroit Auto Show.

Not one to hide from the spotlight, he wanted to imitate some of the great product showmen of his day. He decided to glide into the parking lot right next to the Detroit Convention Center in his 1984 Martin Mercurio turned Fly Car, and then immediately unveil the company's brand-new Fly Car, which would be hidden under a white satin sheet. He had much to pitch: the car's ability to drive or fly, the way it would revolutionize the auto industry even more than electric cars had, and the opportunity it offered for drivers to get back some of their precious leisure time.

Eli's dad was full of charisma and quickly had the media eating out of the palm of his hand. He showed them the splashy five-minute promotional video that he'd previewed with Eli, then concluded the sales session by snapping the satin sheet off the gleaming silver metallic Fly Car like a magician presenting his latest trick.

As the crowd oohed and aahed, a test pilot in an all-black jumpsuit and matching racing helmet opened the door of Fly Car, jumped in, and took off down the crushed red velvet runway and into the chilly January sky.

After watching him soar off, Eli's dad lowered his voice to a whisper while turning back to the admiring throng. "And one more thing: as of last week, Fly Car has been approved by the Federal Aviation Administration. So the future of automobile aviation is here to stay in the Motor City, and it is with Martin Motors!"

Cameras flashed like reflections off a disco ball, and reporters began firing questions at Eli's dad in rapid succession. He had no problem keeping up with them.

"Will there be a special license needed for Fly Car?"

"Yes, but as you can see, you'll more than make up for any time you spend waiting at the DMV, with your shortened daily commute." The reporters laughed.

"What kind of mileage can an owner expect from Fly Car?"

"On planet Earth or in the atmosphere?" The crowd chuckled again. "You can expect approximately thirty miles per gallon on land and roughly fifty miles per gallon while flying."

"Will there ever be a four-seat model of Fly Car?"

"Funny you should mention that. Our research and development department is currently working on answering that exact question."

After answering a few more questions, Eli's dad waved his hands in the air, politely gesturing for the crowd to quiet down.

"I just want to make a few final remarks. I'm aware that the proud people of Detroit have been knocked around a bit this past decade, and I'm hoping that Fly Car will be a green shoot for the city. Someone once said that the cars we drive say a lot about us. It's my deepest hope that we can all say, from this day forward, that we're just a little bit prouder to be Americans. Thank you, everyone, for coming."

Eli's dad stepped down from the podium. As he wove through the crowd of oncoming reporters, he spotted the two people he wanted to see most of all: his wife and son. They met for a group hug, then linked up with Grady, who had been weaving his way through the throng in delight.

"Congratulations, Michael—you've given the city of Detroit a lot of hope today," Grady said.

"And thank you. You reminded me of what's most important in life," Dad said.

"I knew you'd figure it out. You just needed some time."

The four maneuvered through the crowd and made their way toward their waiting sedan and home. Just as Eli was about to get in the car, he noticed Abigail Anderson with her mother. He locked eyes with her for a long moment, and she returned his gaze with a warm smile that melted the chill of the January air. Moments later the sedan was heading to Martin Manor, but the memory brought a smile to his face the entire trip home. And the next morning, Eli woke up to see his dad and Fly Car all over the front page of the *Detroit Free Press*.

Chapter 24

Anybody Seen My Fishing Pole?

The middle school bell rang for the end of the day, and Eli and Murph headed for the school exit as usual. But it wasn't just any day—it was the beginning of spring break. Eli couldn't believe it had been almost a year since the birth of Fly Car. He felt a sense of optimism in the air. Cherry blossoms were blooming on the trees, the weather was warming, and it seemed like there was a very real possibility that he would actually survive sixth grade.

"Look!" Murph said. "It's your dad!"

Eli looked outside and noticed the familiar black luxury sedan waiting for him in the parent carpool line. What was unfamiliar was that Eli's dad was in it, waiting for his son after school for the first time since Eli's first day of kindergarten. Eli did a double take, unsure whether this vision in front of his eyes was real or some sort of crazy dream that he'd always hoped for.

"Catch you later," Murph said. This had been their long-standing joke ever since Eli's miraculous catch in Little League.

Eli's dad opened the door of the familiar black sedan and simply stated, "Get in. I want to show you something."

Fifteen minutes later they were in the city of Detroit. Graffiti-covered walls, broken glass, and boarded-up row houses dotted the city's landscape. Suddenly Eli noticed a series of cranes and construction workers making progress on a nearby building. The picture became clearer. Eli's dad was making good on his promise of renovating the old Packard plant.

"We're hoping to have this building operational in eighteen months. Nine thousand employees will work all three shifts. It's not going to completely save the city, but it's a good start," Dad beamed.

"That's really awesome, Dad!"

"You know what I really want to do right now?"

"I dunno, what?"

"I want to go fishing," Dad said. "Anybody seen my fishing pole?"

"Don't worry, Dad, I can lend you one." Eli gave his dad a wink.

The two of them went down to the barn to retrieve the old wooden rowboat. It was a little dusty, but the vessel still remembered the owner and son who would paddle out to the middle of Old Man Murphy's Pond to participate in their favorite shared hobby. Eli collected the oars and placed them in the hull of the vessel. He always got a smirk out of the sticker cemented to the sidewalls of the boat. "Kiss My Bass," it said.

"You know what the key to fishing is?" Dad smiled.

"Of course—not to startle the fish."

The two hopeful fishermen slowly placed the wooden boat into the water by the wispy green willow tree. A breeze caused the leaves to gently shift in the wind. Eli's dad carefully locked in the oars and slowly paddled past the lily pads and cattails into the center of the pond.

Both father and son baited their hooks and dropped the lines into the water with a plop. The late afternoon sun reflected off the glassy surface of the water. Just then, Eli noticed an afternoon edition of the *Detroit Free Press* rolled up in a tight cylinder at the bottom of the boat. It was today's paper.

He snapped off the teal rubber band. In big black three-inch letters, the front-page headline read, "Michael Martin Takes Leave of Absence from Martin Motors."

"Dad!" Eli said. But his dad only smiled and nodded encouragement at him to read on.

Eli turned back to the newspaper. Mr. Martin would be leaving the company for an indefinite period of time, the article explained, and had named Grady Johnson, co-creator of Fly Car, as interim CEO. Martin Motors was widely considered one of the most successful comeback companies of the year, it noted. The stock price had tripled in the past twelve months, and Fly Car had been the catalyst, generating 70 percent of the company's profits. It was the number-one-selling car in America.

Mr. Martin, the article mentioned, was stepping down as CEO to spend more time with his family.

There was a blissful calm on the pond as Eli placed the newspaper in the side compartment of the boat. He gazed up into the crystal blue sky to see a lemon yellow Fly Car soaring between a pair of puffy white cumulus clouds.

"So why did you do it, Dad?" Eli prodded.

"Do what?" Dad asked, pretending naïveté.

"Step down from being CEO. Duh," Eli joked.

"I just decided that I'd rather make a hundred—no, make that a thousand—times less money, and be a thousand times happier." He reached over and softly patted his only child's head.

Just then, he felt a tug on his pole. The rod arched like a candy cane at Christmas. "Nice day to go fishing," Dad said. "I've got the net—you bring him in, son."

At that moment Eli felt, for the first time in a long while, that he was finally home.

John Fuller is an elementary school teacher in Menlo Park, California, where he lives with his wife, Jacquelline, and their two daughters, Hosanna and Sophie. He is also a proud owner of a Pomeranian, Teddy. *Fly Car* was created to draw families closer together, to encourage kids to dream big and chase their moments of inspiration.

Shane Burke lives in Northern California and has been drawing and painting since he could hold a pencil. He took private art lessons when he was young and began winning awards and contests by the age of seven. His first big commission came at age nine when he created artwork for a billboard near his hometown of Tracy, California. His greatest influences came from his grandfather and elementary school teachers. He loved watching his grandfather paint landscapes and wanted to be just like him. Shane is a creative daydreamer who is at complete peace when putting ink to paper. To see more of his work, visit www.beezink.com.

Acknowledgments

First off, I want to thank God for giving me the inspiration and endurance to complete this project. Special thanks to Nick Van Santen and Rich Butler, who were early editors on *Fly Car*. Your feedback was invaluable and provided the right combination of encouragement and critique. Your input kept me motivated to write, revise, and sharpen the storyline.

Thank you to my wife, Jacquelline, who has always inspired me to be the best version of myself that I could possibly be. I didn't always know what shape that me would take, but I am appreciative. A shout-out to my mom, Anne Fuller, who continues to amaze me with her joy throughout every season of her life; my father, Gary "Cappy" Fuller, for his amazing stories of flying airplanes; my older brother, Robert, who was the Murph in my life watching over me as a kid; my younger brother, Andrew, whose entrepreneurial spirit gave me the courage to dream about writing a children's book; and my editor, Melanie Light, for her timely feedback and encouragement to move *Fly Car* forward the final 10 percent.

Special thanks to my illustrator, Shane Burke, for translating the words of *Fly Car* into beautiful shape and form; and to my line editor, Sherri Schultz, for turning my drafts into a manuscript that was worthy of being published. Warm fuzzies to my fourth-grade class, who allowed me to read a draft version of *Fly Car* to them and cheered anyway. Finally, much love to Hosanna and Sophie, who turned a cranky old man into a softy.

Ten-year-old Eli Martin would do just about anything to spend more time with his dad. But Dad's working overtime to save Martin Motors, the family's struggling car company. One day Eli and his best friend, Earl, stumble on a classic cherry red sports car produced by Martin Motors back in 1984, hidden away in the family's barn.

Eli starts to wonder: What if the red sports car could actually fly? A car like that could save his dad's company—and send their relationship soaring to new heights. With the help of his family's faithful groundskeeper, Grady, Eli starts to put his plan into action.

16544007R00123

Made in the USA
San Bernardino, CA
07 November 2014